The Diagram Group

HUMAN GEOGRAPHY in DIAGRAMS

General Editor: Michael Morrish
Head of Geography, Alleyn's School, London

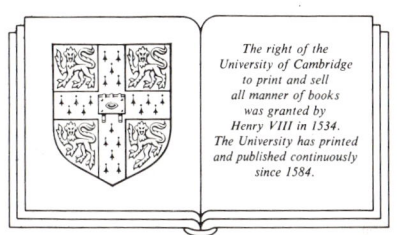

Cambridge University Press

Cambridge

London   New York   New Rochelle

Melbourne   Sydney

General Editor: Michael Morrish
Research: Tom Heap
Editorial Assistant: Annabel Else
Artists: Joe Bonello, Alastair Burnside, Brian Hewson, Philip Patenall, Paula Preston
Index: David Harding

Published by the Press Syndicate of the University of Cambridge
The Pitt Building, Trumpington Street, Cambridge CB2 1RP
32 East 57th Street, New York, NY 10022, USA
10 Stamford Road, Oakleigh, Melbourne 3166, Australia

© Diagram Visual Information Ltd 1986

First published 1986

Printed in Great Britain by Technographic Design & Print

British Library Cataloguing in Publication Data

Diagram Group
   Human geography in diagrams.
   1. Anthropo-geography
   I. Title
   304.2   GF41

ISBN 0-521-31137-8

Foreword

Human Geography in Diagrams is a resource book for geographers of all levels. It contains over 100 'master' diagrams which have been carefully drawn to ensure that they can be easily and clearly reproduced on even the most modest photocopier. The diagrams in this book can be used to supplement any human geography course. As the illustrations vary in their complexity, some will be most appropriate for use with lower secondary students, while others will be more useful to 'GCSE' or 'A' level candidates.

The book is divided into nine major sections: population, settlement, urban geography, agriculture, industry, energy, transport, economic development and environment.

Each diagram can be used as an integral part of a course or lesson, the clarity of the drawing being used to help the students' understanding of the subject. Alternatively, the worksheets can supplement text books and the students' notes, becoming a reference and revision aid. Moreover, the diagrams have been designed so that, by masking out either the keys or the captions, they can be used for tests or as examination illustrations. Finally, the labelling is minimal so as to allow maximum flexibility in teaching and shading is only added for clarity.

The end result is a collection of practical and stimulating worksheets which will assist and enhance students' understanding of human geography.

CONTENTS

SECTION 1: POPULATION

SECTION 2: SETTLEMENT

SECTION 3: URBAN GEOGRAPHY

3.1 World urbanisation: distribution of million cities
3.2 City land use: comparison of developed and developing cities
Leeds
Delhi
3.3 Land use and land values in Western cities
City plan and land value graph
Cross section through a typical city
3.4 Models of urban structure
Concentric theory (after Burgess)
Sector theory (after Hoyt and Davie)
Multiple nuclei theory (after Harris and Ullman)
3.5 A model of industrial location in a city
3.6 Contrasts in the inner city: the central business district and the inner city
3.7 World urbanisation: proportion of city dwellers
3.8 Housing styles
Country cottage; Georgian mansion; Georgian terrace; Nineteenth century terrace; Inter-war housing; 'Stockbroker belt' private housing; High-rise blocks of flats; Modern suburban housing estate; Modern city apartment

SECTION 4: AGRICULTURE

4.1 Factors influencing agricultural activity
Environmental, social, technological, economic, personal
4.2 World distribution of major types of agriculture
Modern mixed farm in developed country
Crop based, livestock-based, mixed farming
4.3 Farm types
Mixed farming
Intensive monoculture
Extensive grazing
Rice paddies
4.4 Distribution of major agricultural crops
4.5 Farm tools and machinery
Basic
Intermediate
Mechanised
4.6 The changing farmscape in developed countries
Thirty years ago; Today
4.7 Agricultural intensity and land use patterns
The von Thünen model and its modifications
4.8 World fishing: major grounds, catch and methods
Drifting, trawling; purse seining

SECTION 5: INDUSTRY

5.1 Factors influencing industrial location
5.2 World manufacturing regions and major sources of industrial raw materials
5.3 World employment structure
Comparison of primary, secondary and tertiary employment in a selection of countries
5.4 Primary industry: a modern coalmine
5.5 Heavy manufacturing: iron and steel making
5.6 Assembly industry: car production
5.7 A major enclosed shopping centre: Brent Cross in North London

POPULATION
World distribution of population

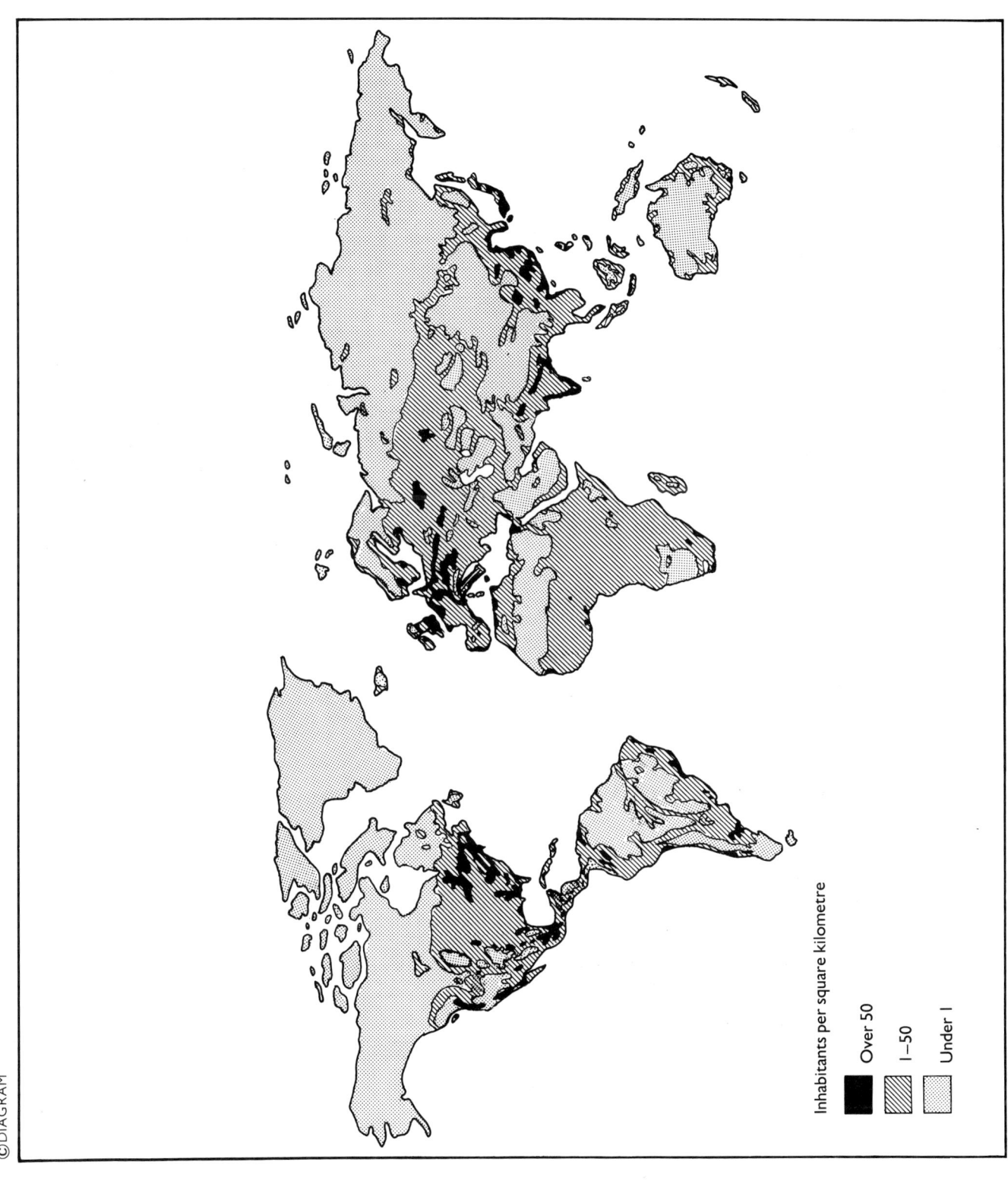

Inhabitants per square kilometre

◼ Over 50

▨ 1–50

░ Under 1

POPULATION
Patterns of population increase

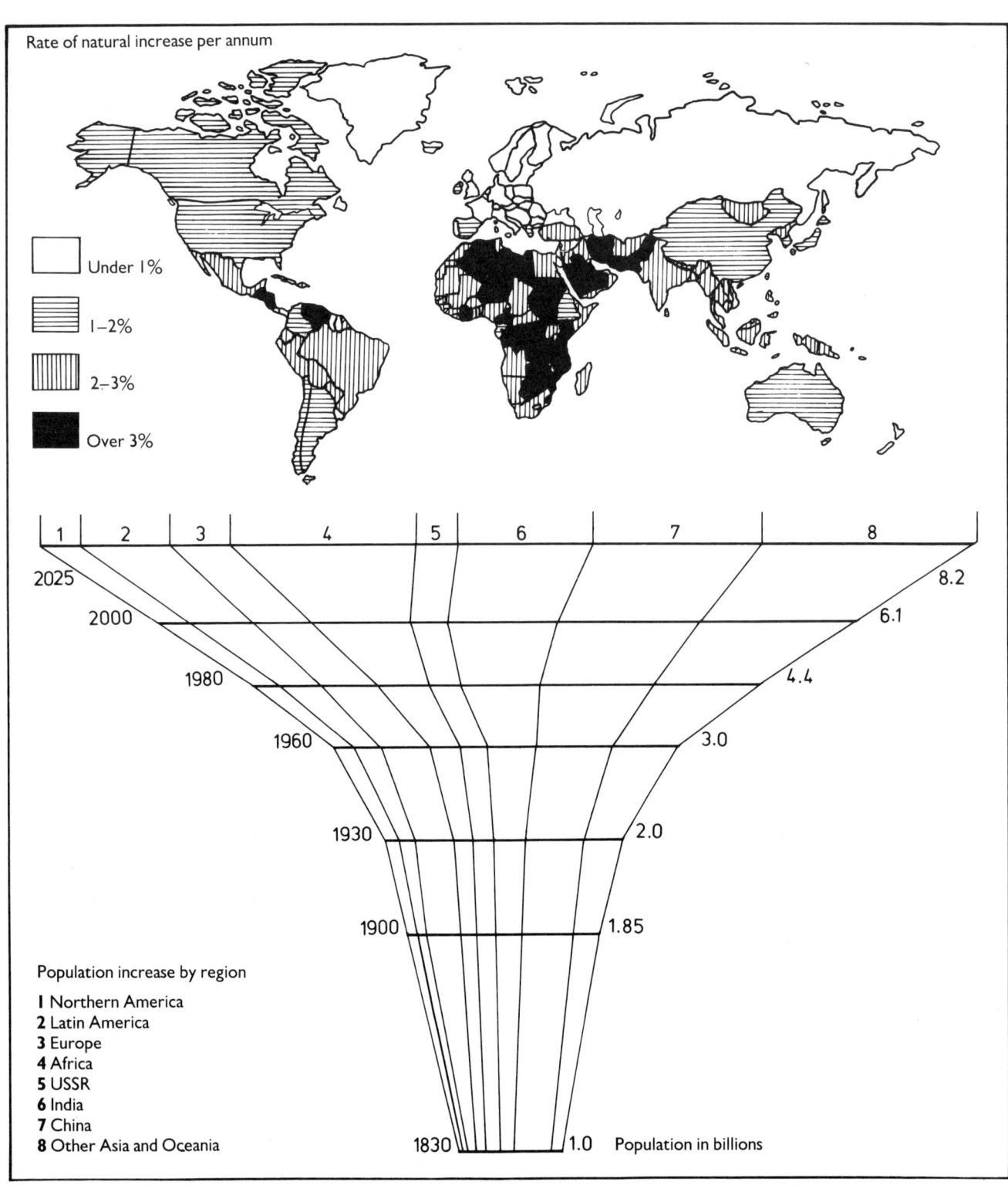

Rate of natural increase per annum

Under 1%

1–2%

2–3%

Over 3%

2025   8.2

2000   6.1

1980   4.4

1960   3.0

1930   2.0

1900   1.85

1830   1.0   Population in billions

Population increase by region

1 Northern America
2 Latin America
3 Europe
4 Africa
5 USSR
6 India
7 China
8 Other Asia and Oceania

© DIAGRAM

POPULATION
Birth rates, death rates and natural increase

—·—· **1** Birth rate per 1000
——— **2** Death rate per 1000

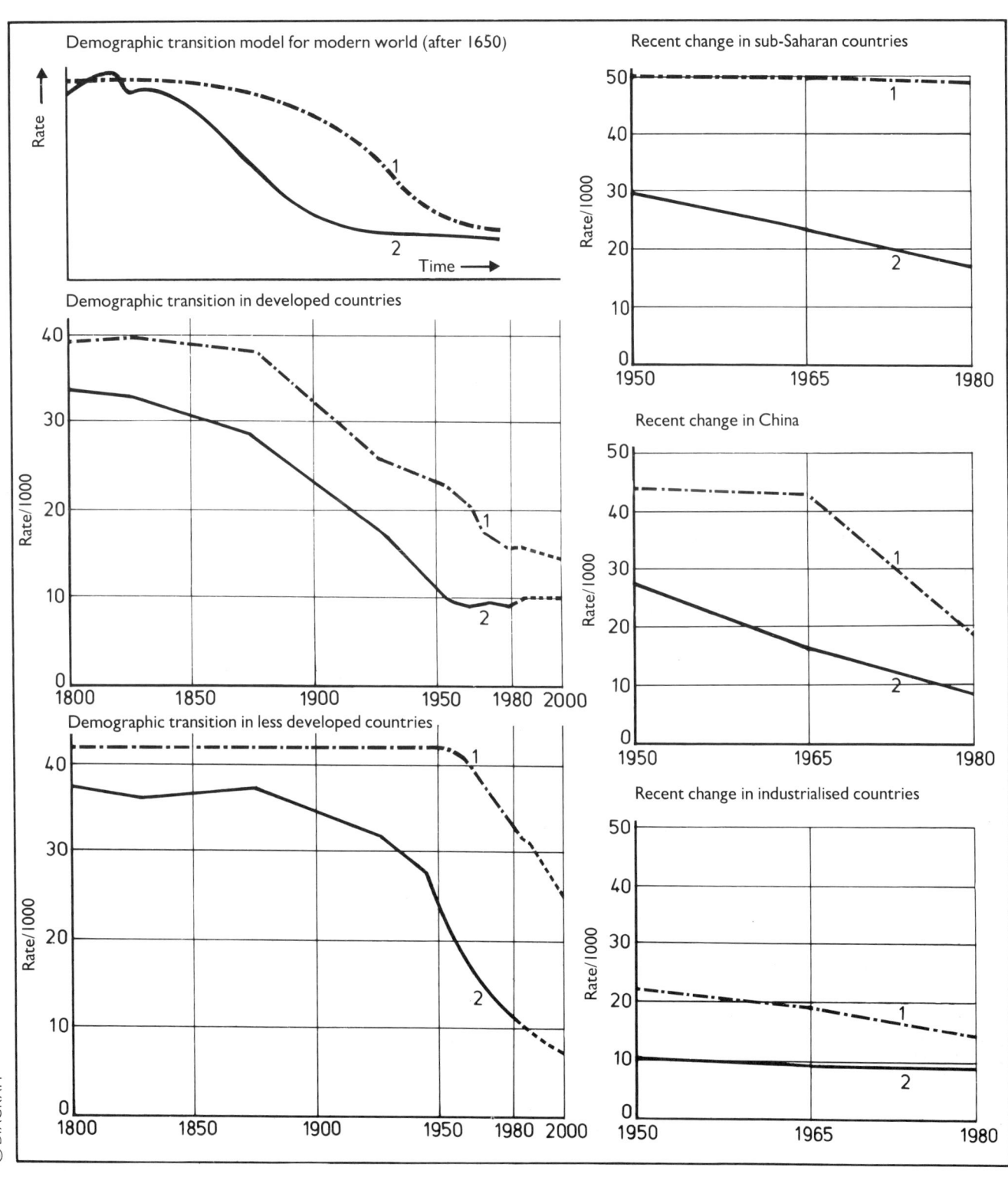

Demographic transition model for modern world (after 1650)

Rate
Time

Recent change in sub-Saharan countries

Demographic transition in developed countries

Recent change in China

Demographic transition in less developed countries

Recent change in industrialised countries

© DIAGRAM

POPULATION
Life expectancy

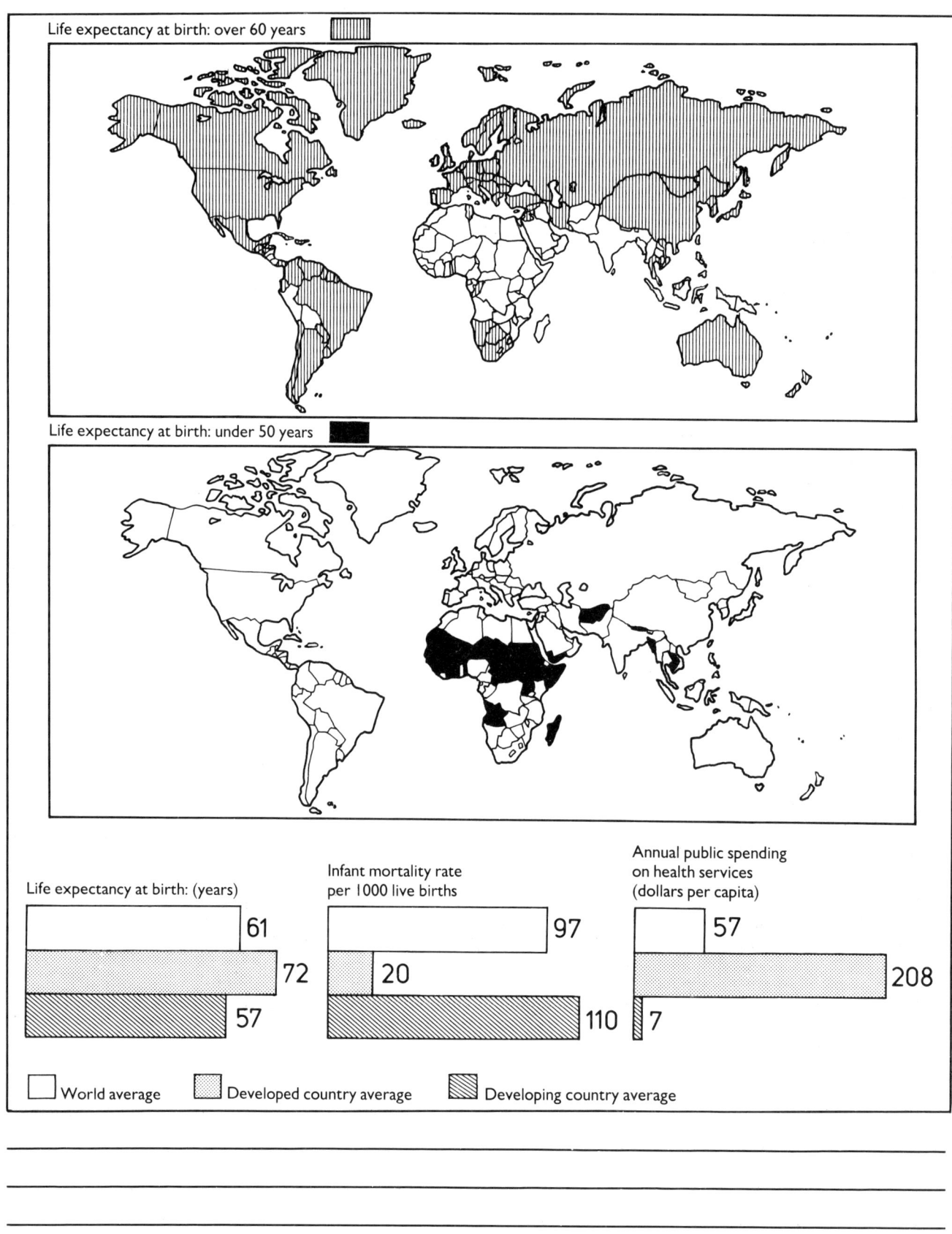

Life expectancy at birth: over 60 years

Life expectancy at birth: under 50 years

Life expectancy at birth: (years)
61
72
57

Infant mortality rate per 1000 live births
97
20
110

Annual public spending on health services (dollars per capita)
57
208
7

☐ World average   ▨ Developed country average   ▨ Developing country average

©DIAGRAM

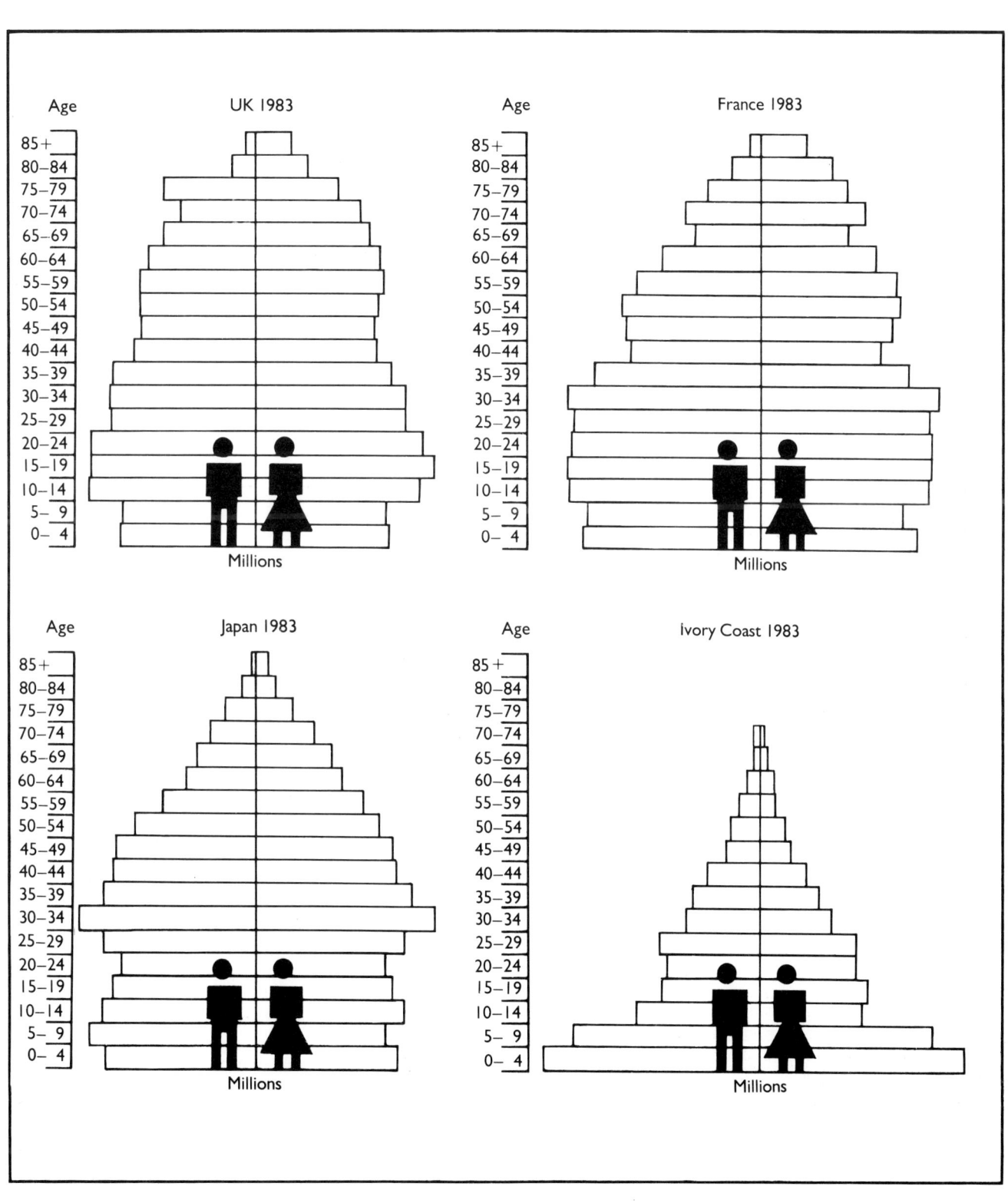

POPULATION
Types and patterns of migration

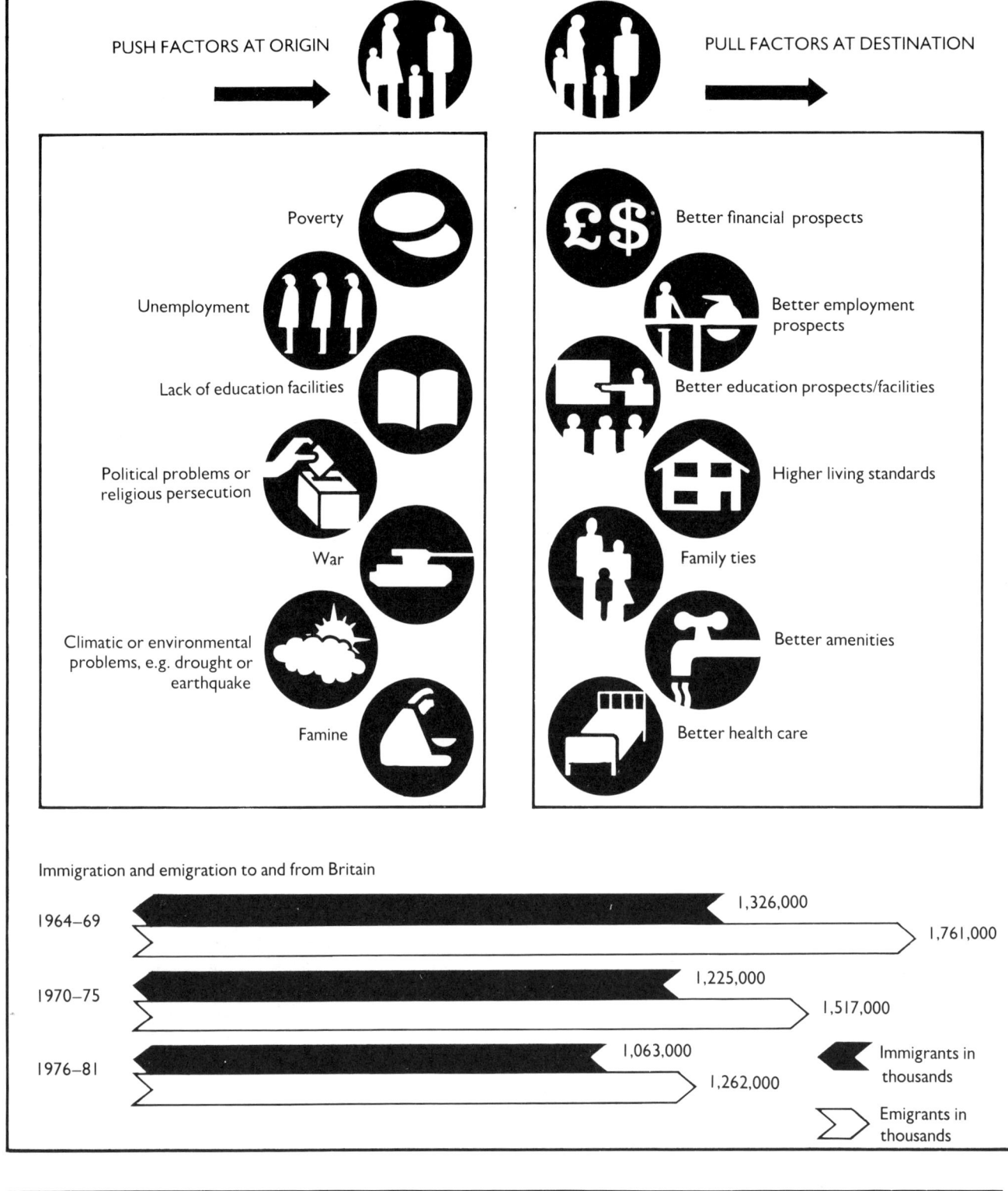

PUSH FACTORS AT ORIGIN

PULL FACTORS AT DESTINATION

Poverty

Unemployment

Lack of education facilities

Political problems or religious persecution

War

Climatic or environmental problems, e.g. drought or earthquake

Famine

Better financial prospects

Better employment prospects

Better education prospects/facilities

Higher living standards

Family ties

Better amenities

Better health care

Immigration and emigration to and from Britain

1964–69   1,326,000   1,761,000

1970–75   1,225,000   1,517,000

1976–81   1,063,000   1,262,000

Immigrants in thousands

Emigrants in thousands

© DIAGRAM

SETTLEMENT
Typical settlement sites and forms

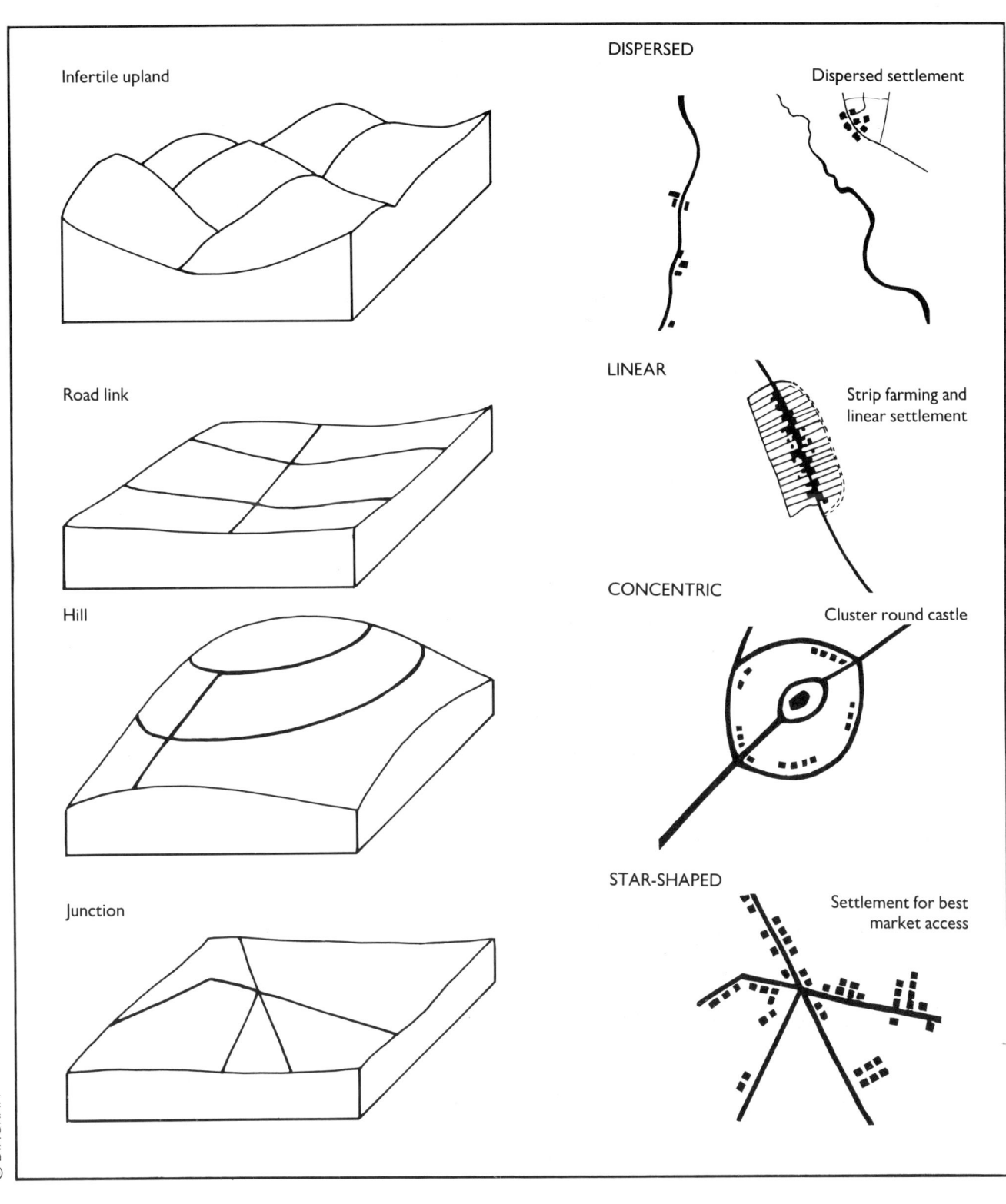

Infertile upland

Road link

Hill

Junction

DISPERSED

Dispersed settlement

LINEAR

Strip farming and linear settlement

CONCENTRIC

Cluster round castle

STAR-SHAPED

Settlement for best market access

© DIAGRAM

Clustered

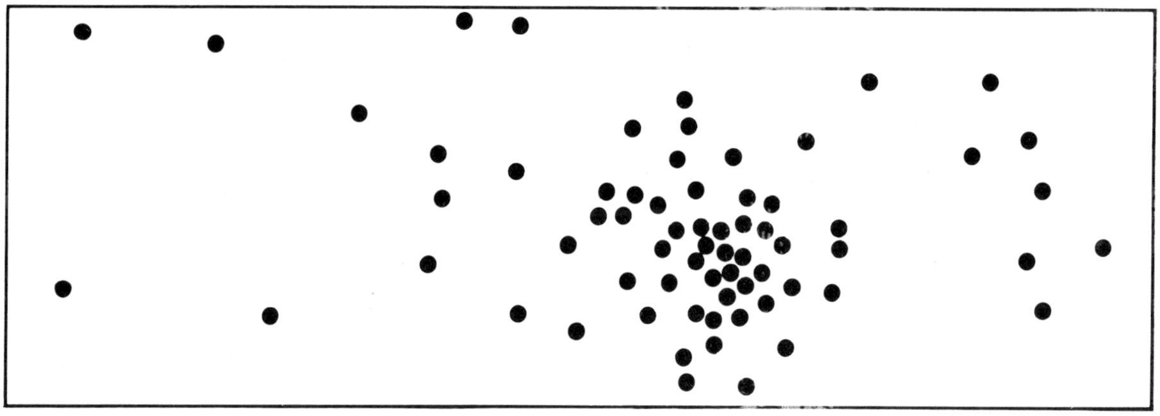

Regular dispersed

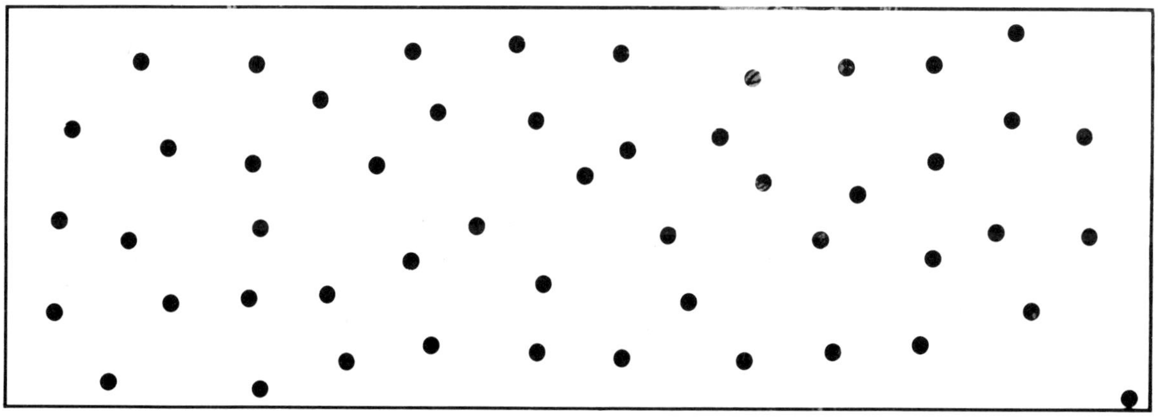

Random

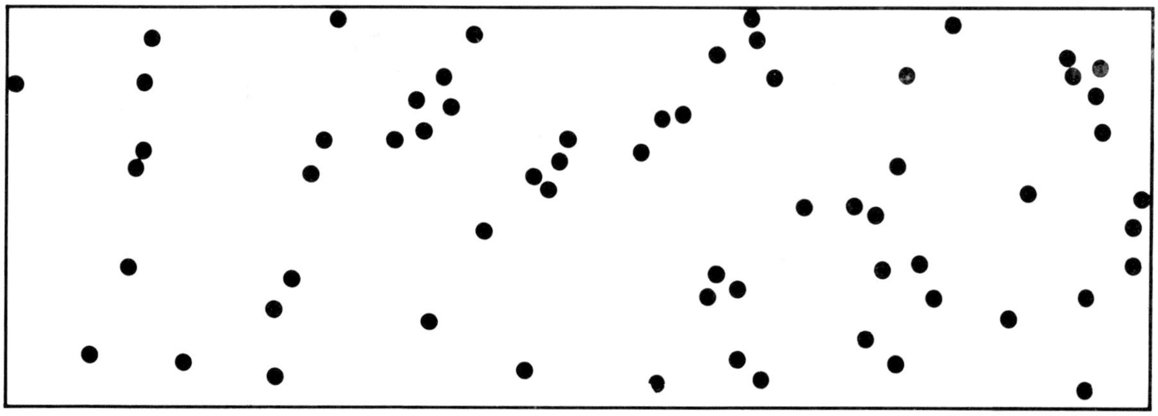

SETTLEMENT
Settlement size and functions

● Major regional centre   ● Local centre

● Area centre

Spheres of influence

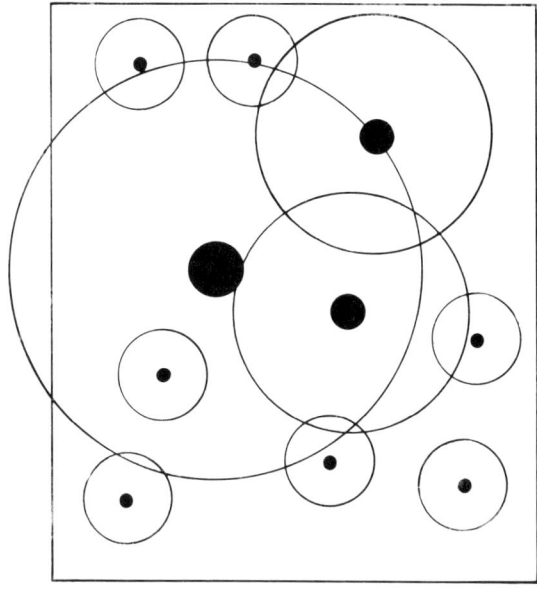

Main transport routes

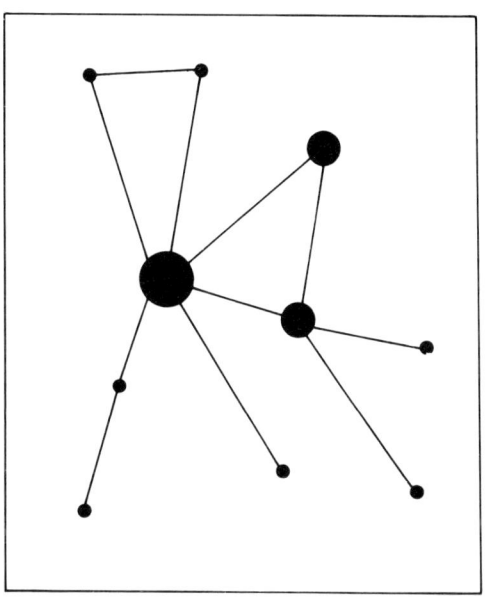

Desire lines for grocery shopping

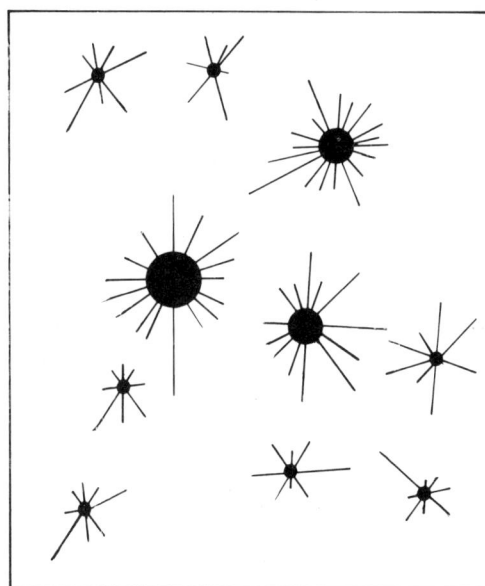

Desire lines for furniture shopping

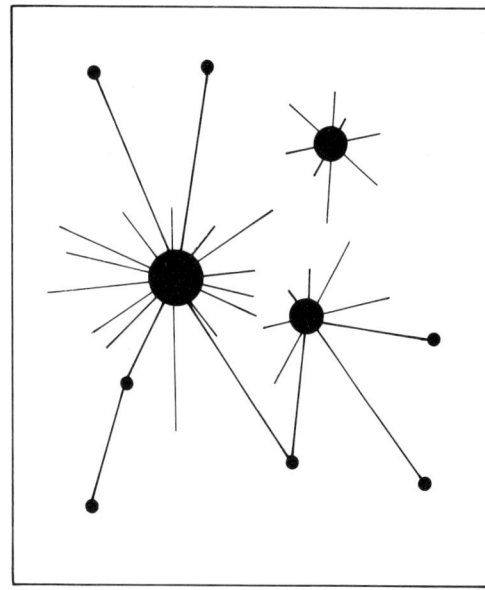

© DIAGRAM

● Market town
• Village
. Hamlet

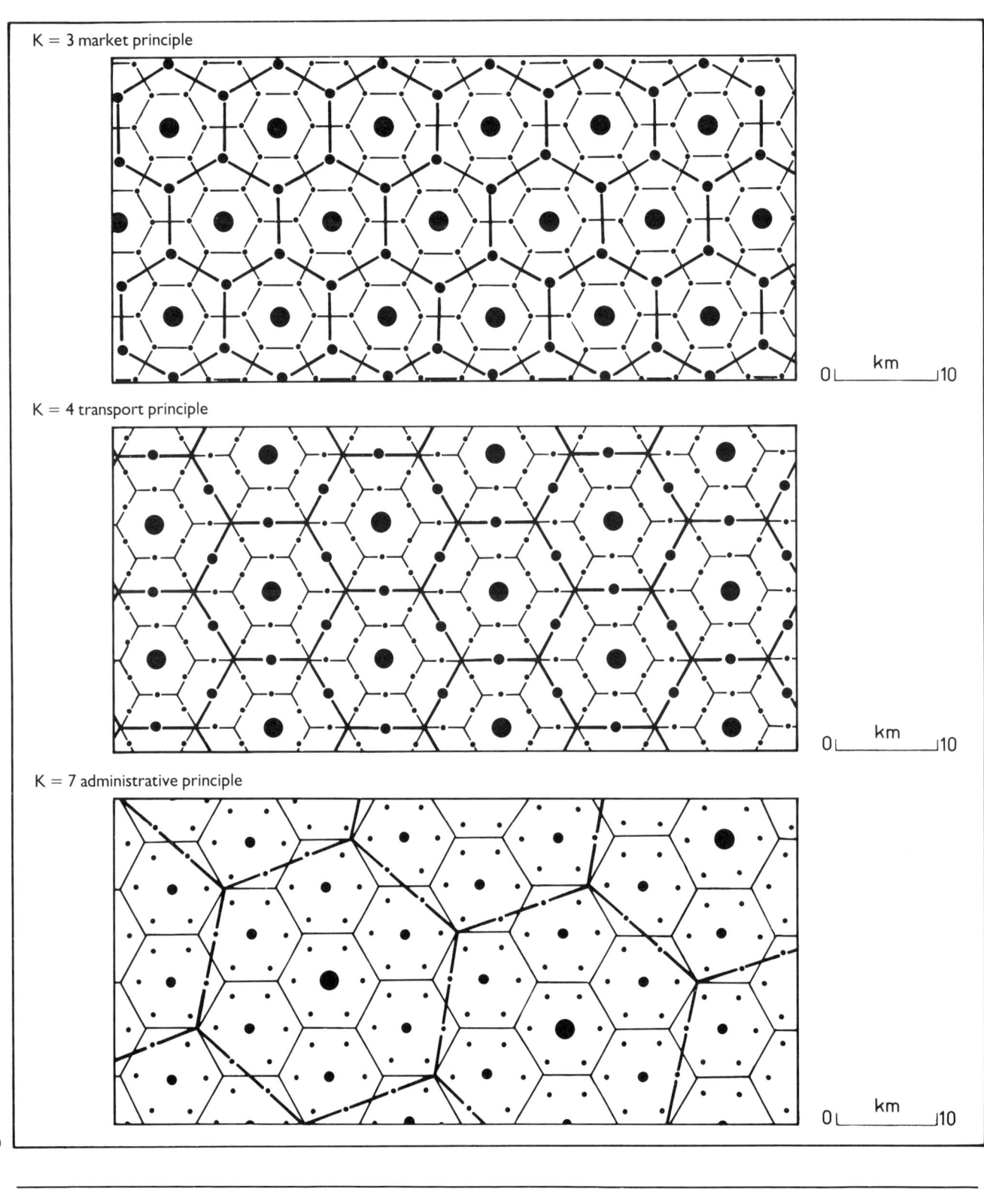

K = 3 market principle

0 | km | 10

K = 4 transport principle

0 | km | 10

K = 7 administrative principle

0 | km | 10

© DIAGRAM

—— 1950
– – 1975
······· 2000

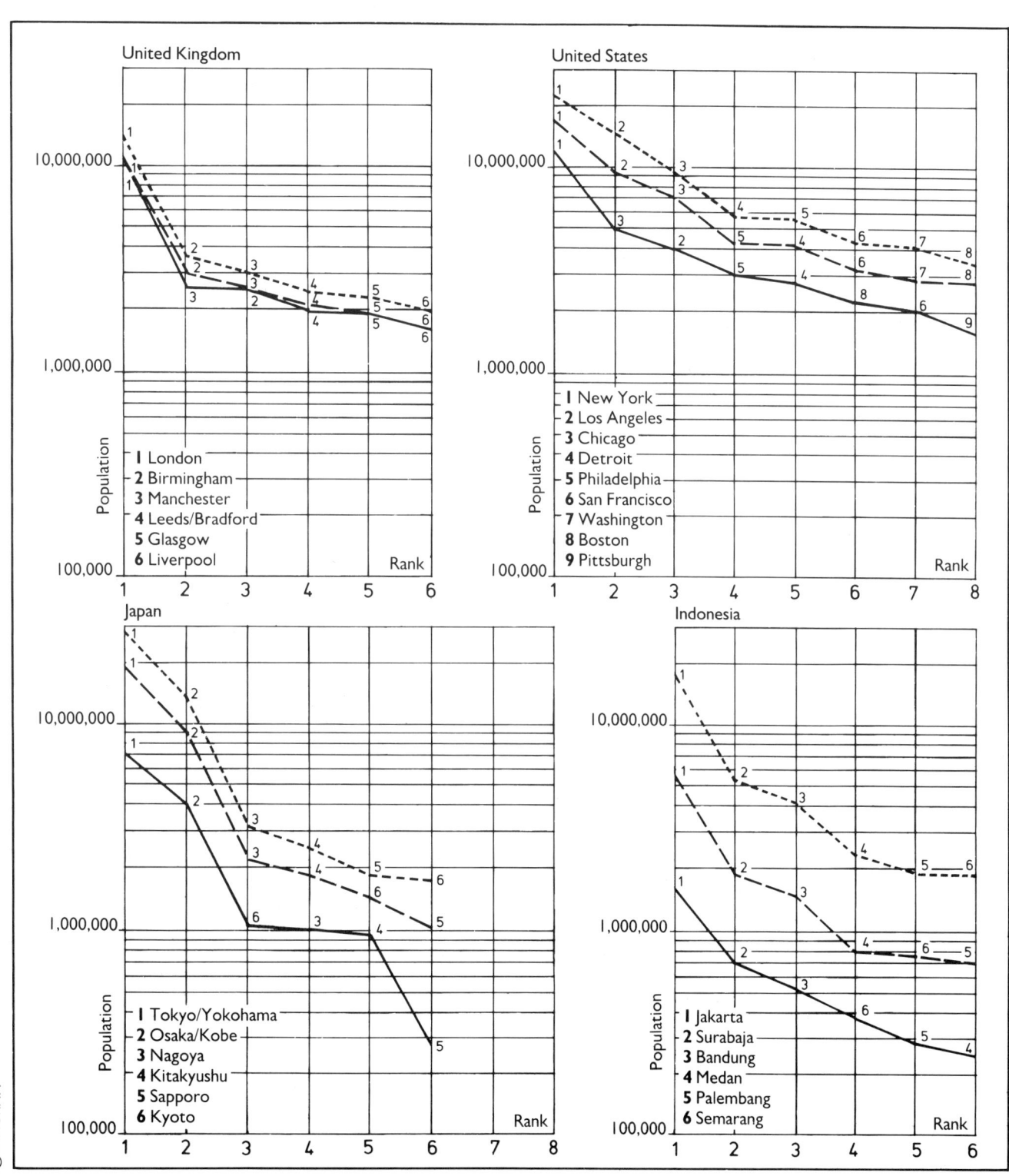

SETTLEMENT
The changing village

Medieval

Nineteenth century

Modern

©DIAGRAM

World urbanisation: the distribution of million cities

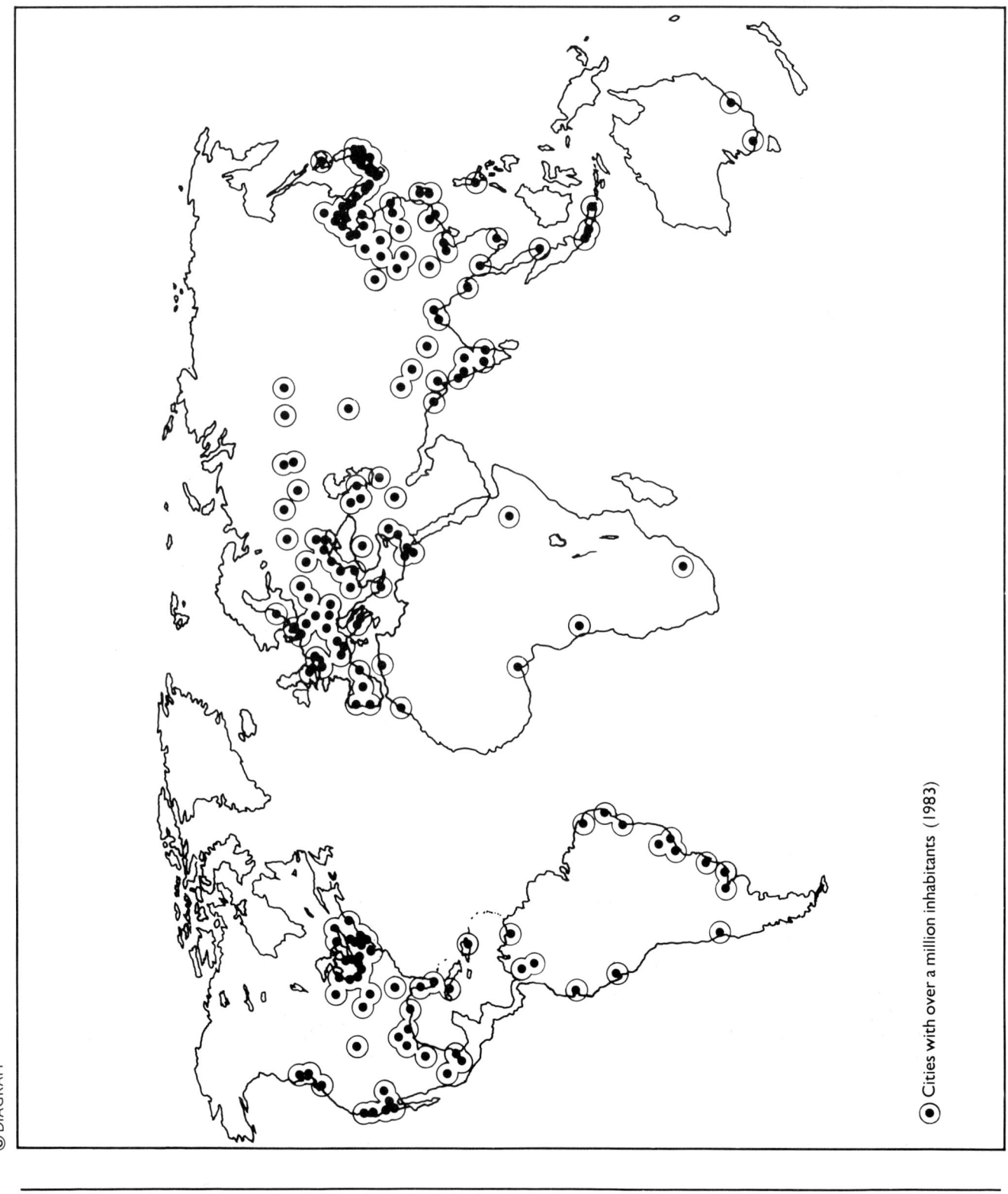

⊙ Cities with over a million inhabitants (1983)

City land use: comparison of developed and developing cities

Leeds

- CBD
- Parks and open space
- Industry
- Housing Built pre 1918
- Built 1918–45
- Built post 1945

0 — 3
km

Delhi

- CBD
- Parks and open space
- Industry
- Housing Built pre 1947
- Built post 1947
- ✈ Airfield
- **1** Old city centre
- **2** New city centre

0 — 3
km

Land use and land values in western cities

City plan and land value graph

Rateable value (£ per square front foot)

1 C.B.D: shops, offices and entertainment
2 Inner city residential, old terraces, old industry and warehousing
3 Middle-class residential, apartment blocks, light industry and suburban housing
4 Middle and high-class residential

©DIAGRAM

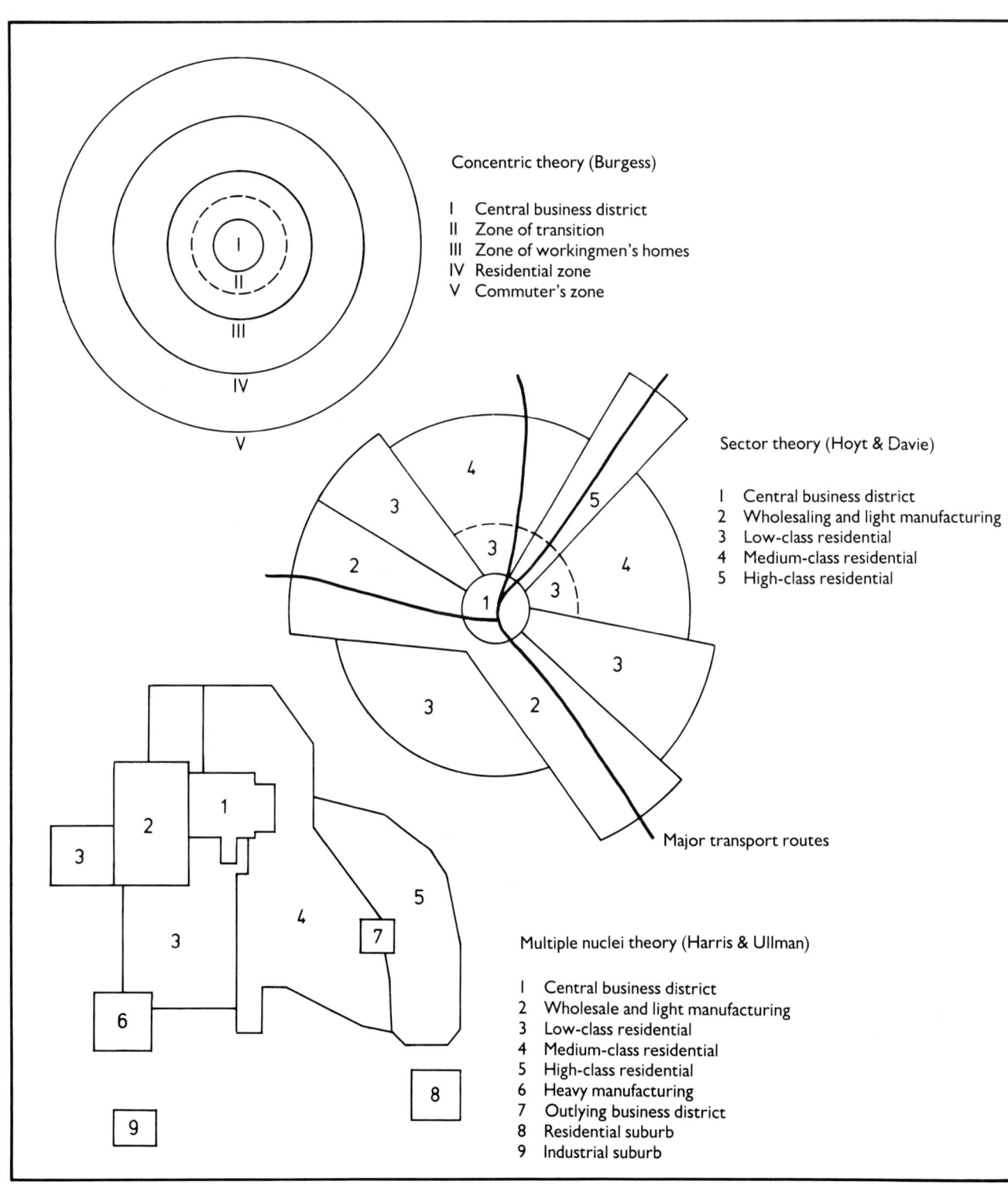

Concentric theory (Burgess)

I Central business district
II Zone of transition
III Zone of workingmen's homes
IV Residential zone
V Commuter's zone

Sector theory (Hoyt & Davie)

I Central business district
2 Wholesaling and light manufacturing
3 Low-class residential
4 Medium-class residential
5 High-class residential

Major transport routes

Multiple nuclei theory (Harris & Ullman)

I Central business district
2 Wholesale and light manufacturing
3 Low-class residential
4 Medium-class residential
5 High-class residential
6 Heavy manufacturing
7 Outlying business district
8 Residential suburb
9 Industrial suburb

©DIAGRAM

Model of industrial location in a city

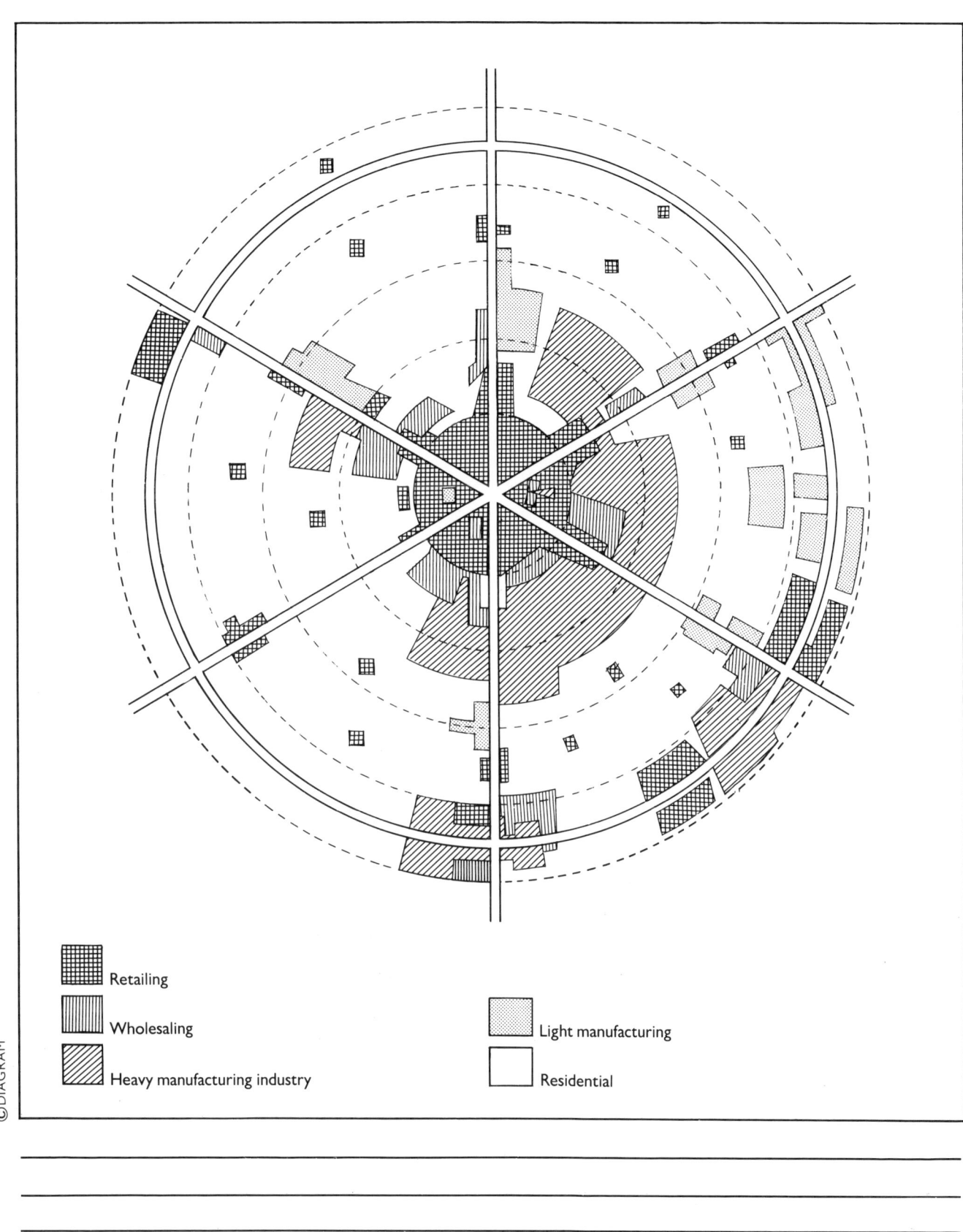

Retailing

Wholesaling

Heavy manufacturing industry

Light manufacturing

Residential

URBAN GEOGRAPHY
Contrasts in the inner city

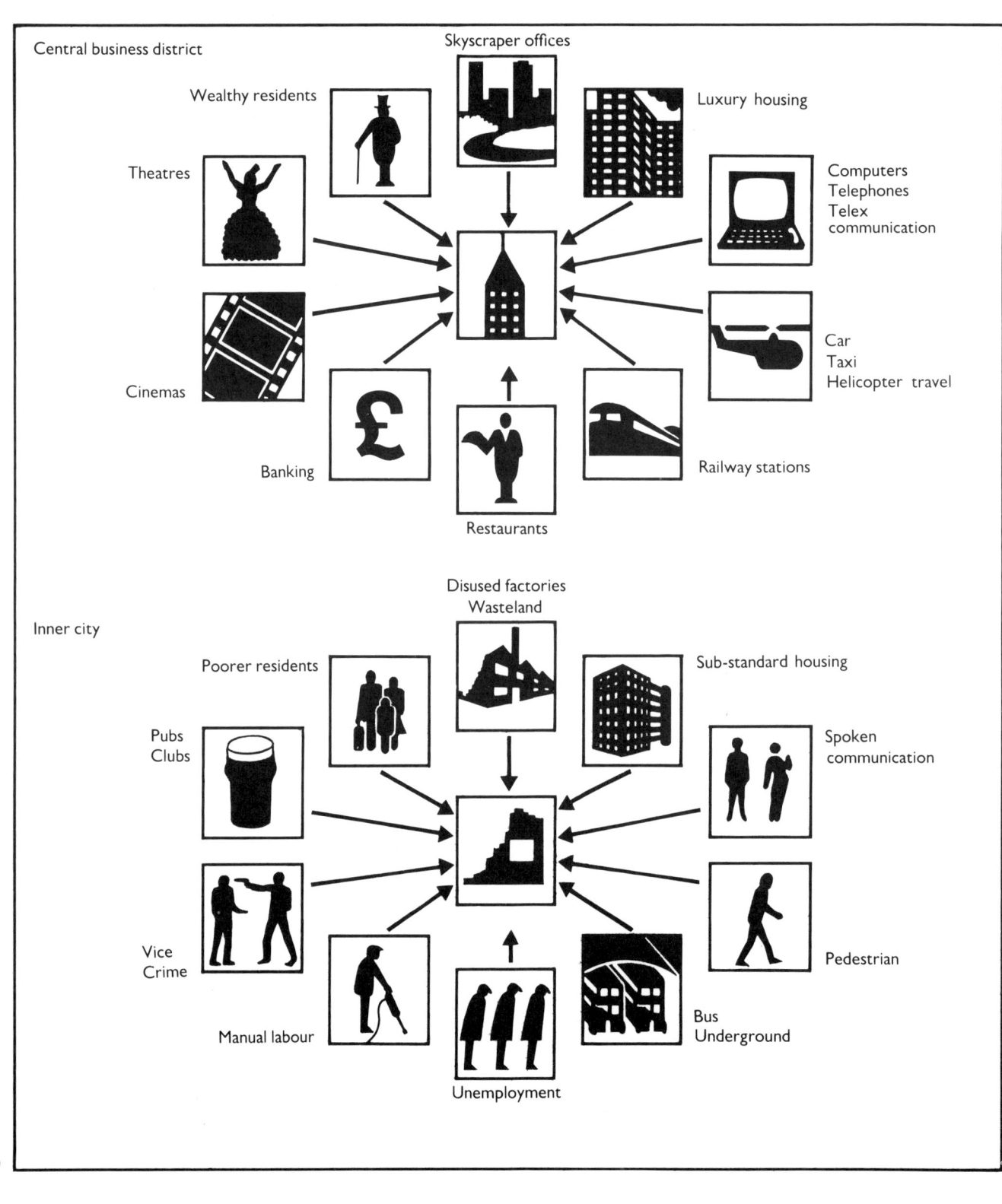

Central business district

Skyscraper offices

Wealthy residents

Luxury housing

Theatres

Computers
Telephones
Telex
communication

Cinemas

Car
Taxi
Helicopter travel

Banking

Restaurants

Railway stations

Inner city

Disused factories
Wasteland

Poorer residents

Sub-standard housing

Pubs
Clubs

Spoken
communication

Vice
Crime

Pedestrian

Manual labour

Bus
Underground

Unemployment

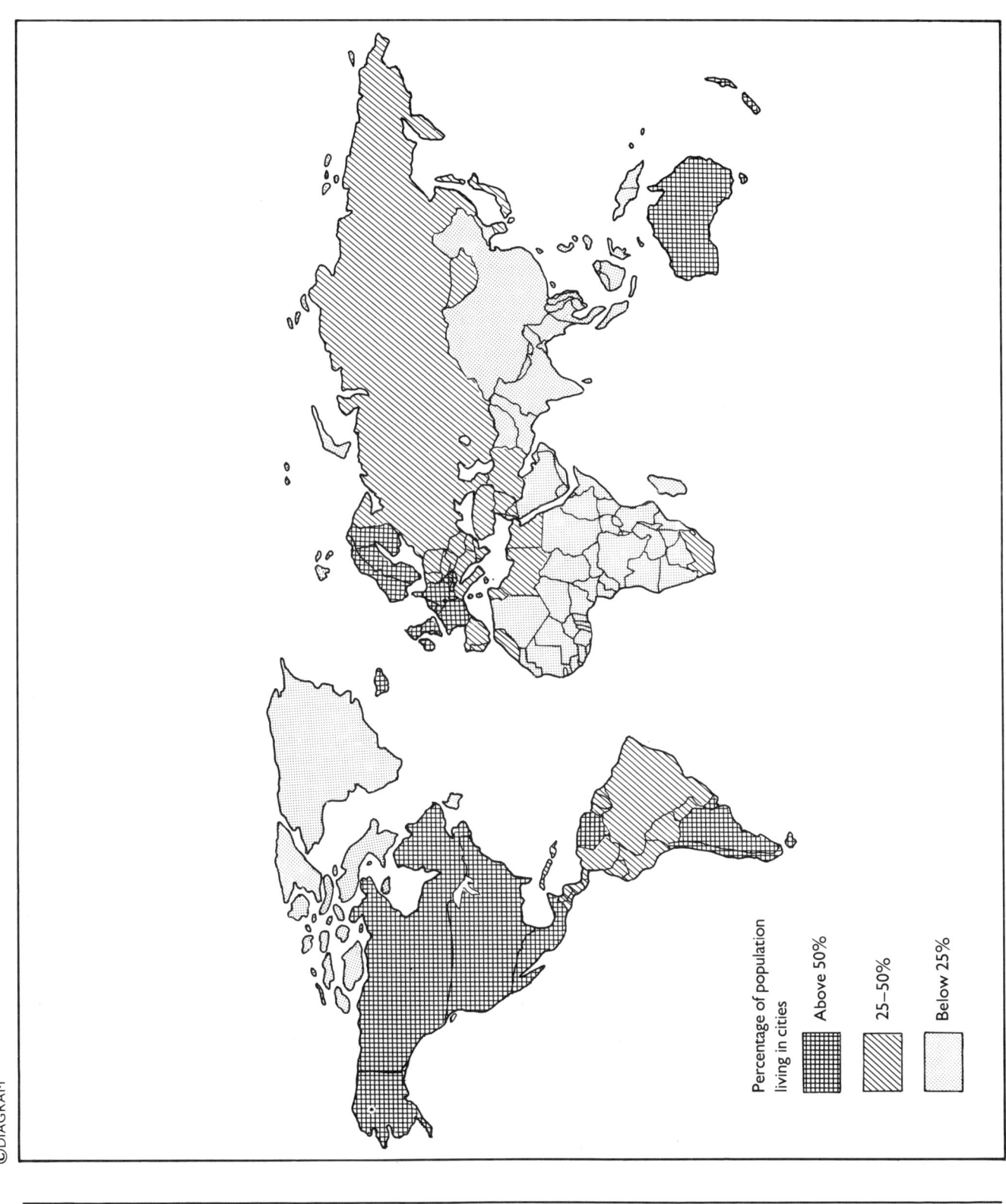

Percentage of population
living in cities

Above 50%

25–50%

Below 25%

©DIAGRAM

Country cottage

Georgian mansion

Georgian terrace

Nineteenth century terrace

Inter-war suburban housing

'Stockbroker belt' private housing

High-rise blocks of flats

Modern suburban housing estate

Modern city apartment

AGRICULTURE
Factors influencing agricultural activity

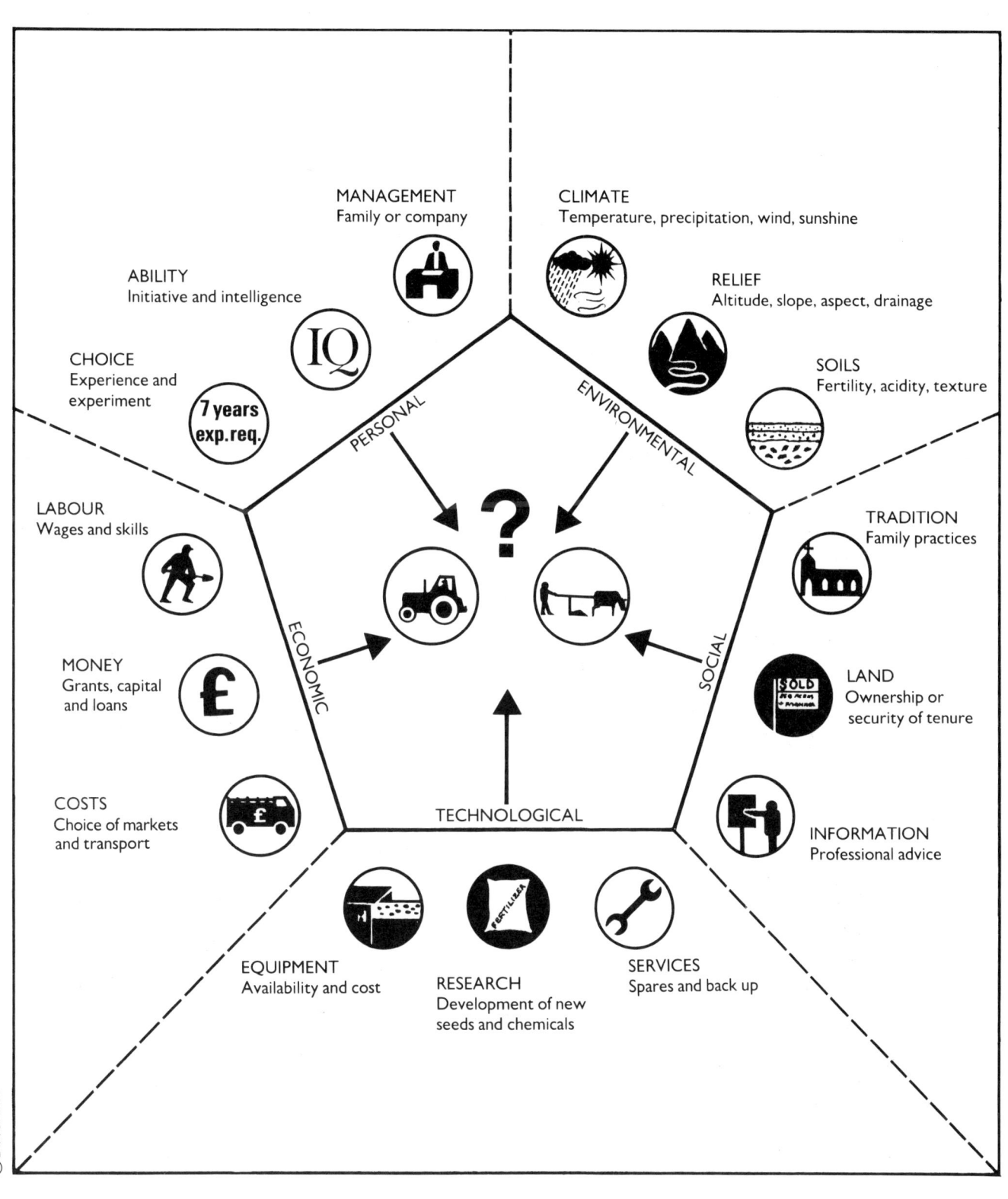

World distribution of major types of agriculture

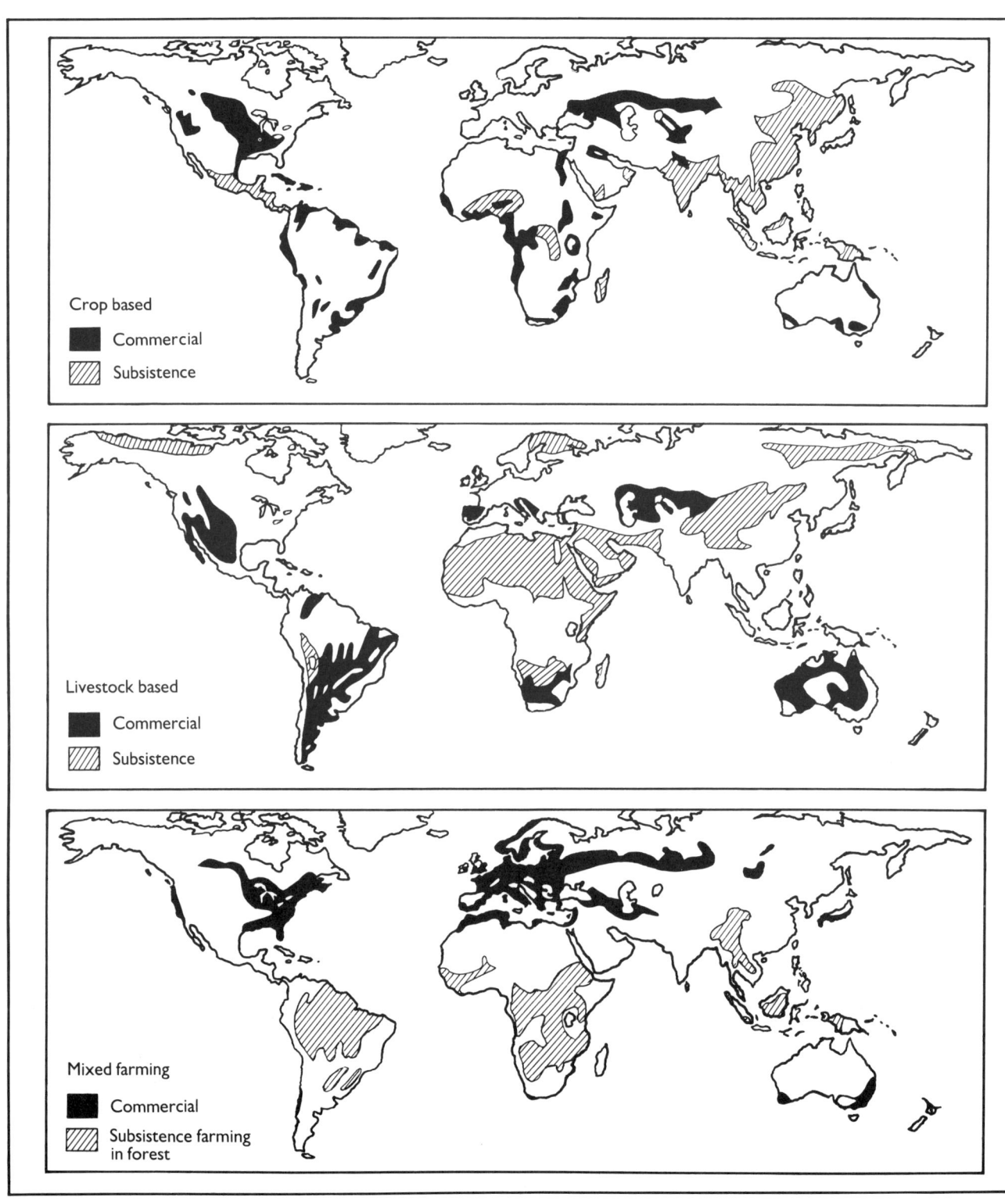

Crop based

■ Commercial

▨ Subsistence

Livestock based

■ Commercial

▨ Subsistence

Mixed farming

■ Commercial

▨ Subsistence farming
in forest

©DIAGRAM

Farm types

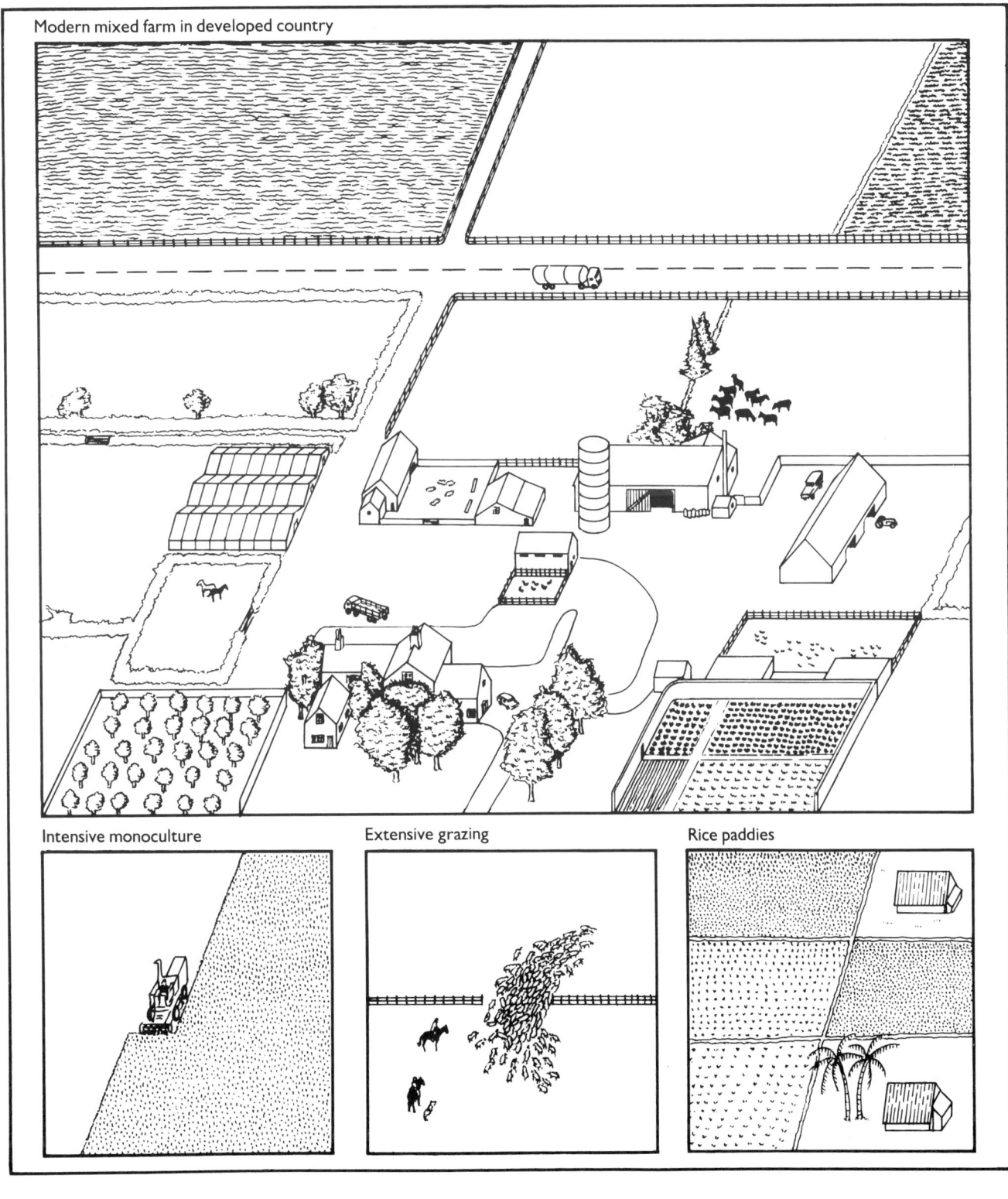

Modern mixed farm in developed country

Intensive monoculture

Extensive grazing

Rice paddies

©DIAGRAM

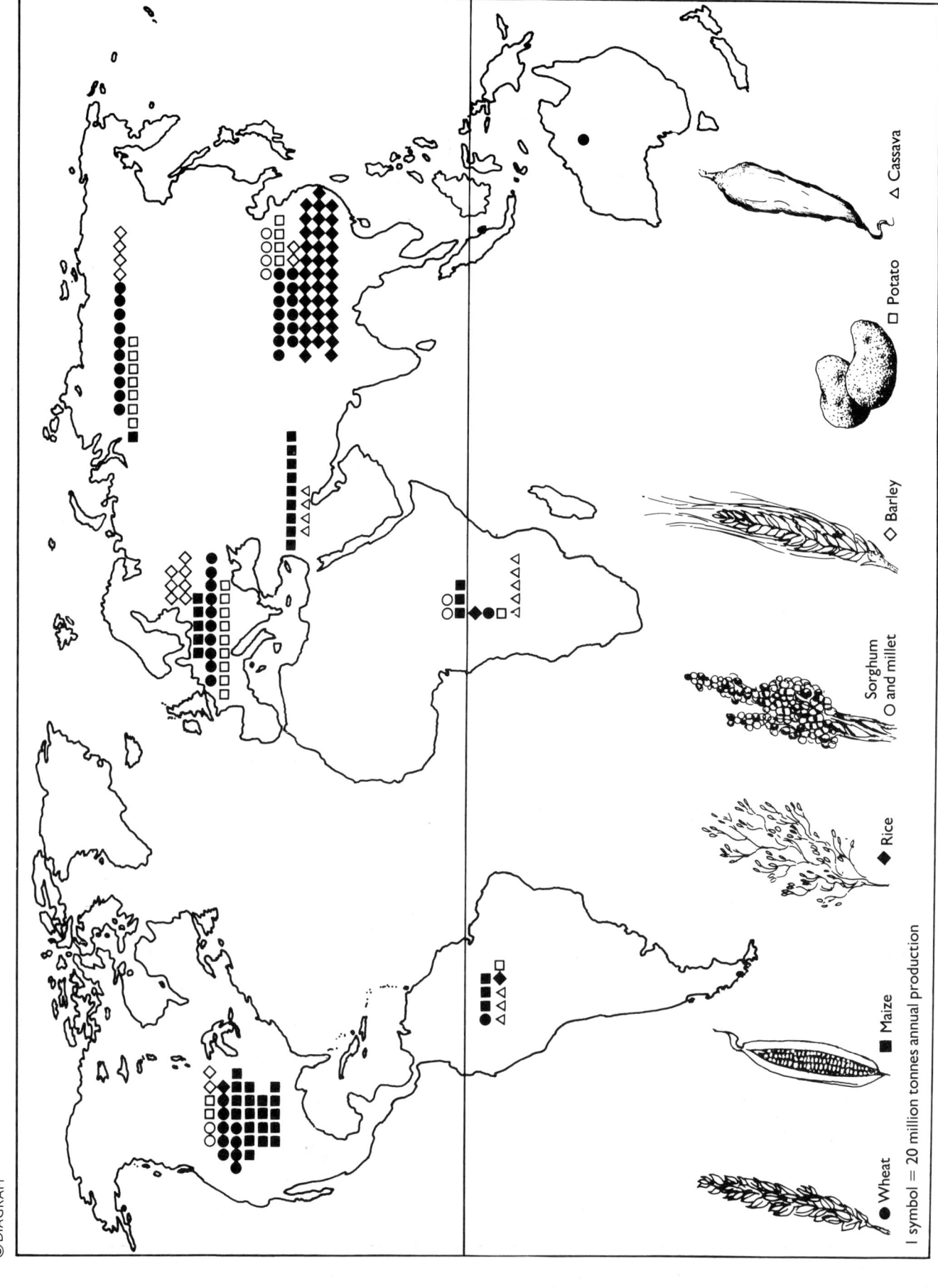

△ Cassava

□ Potato

◇ Barley

Sorghum
○ and millet

◆ Rice

■ Maize

● Wheat

1 symbol = 20 million tonnes annual production

©DIAGRAM

AGRICULTURE
Farming tools and machinery

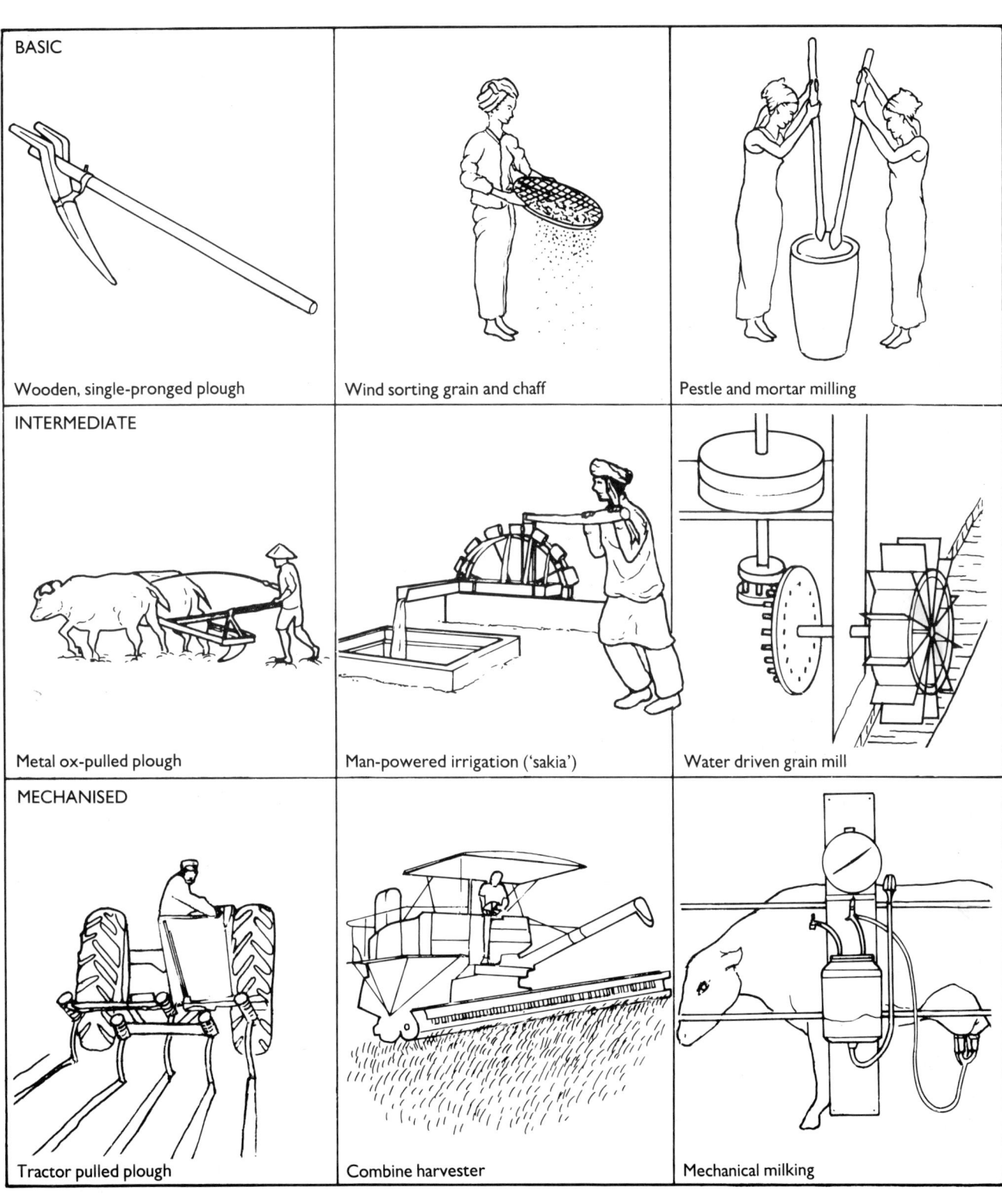

BASIC

Wooden, single-pronged plough

Wind sorting grain and chaff

Pestle and mortar milling

INTERMEDIATE

Metal ox-pulled plough

Man-powered irrigation ('sakia')

Water driven grain mill

MECHANISED

Tractor pulled plough

Combine harvester

Mechanical milking

© DIAGRAM

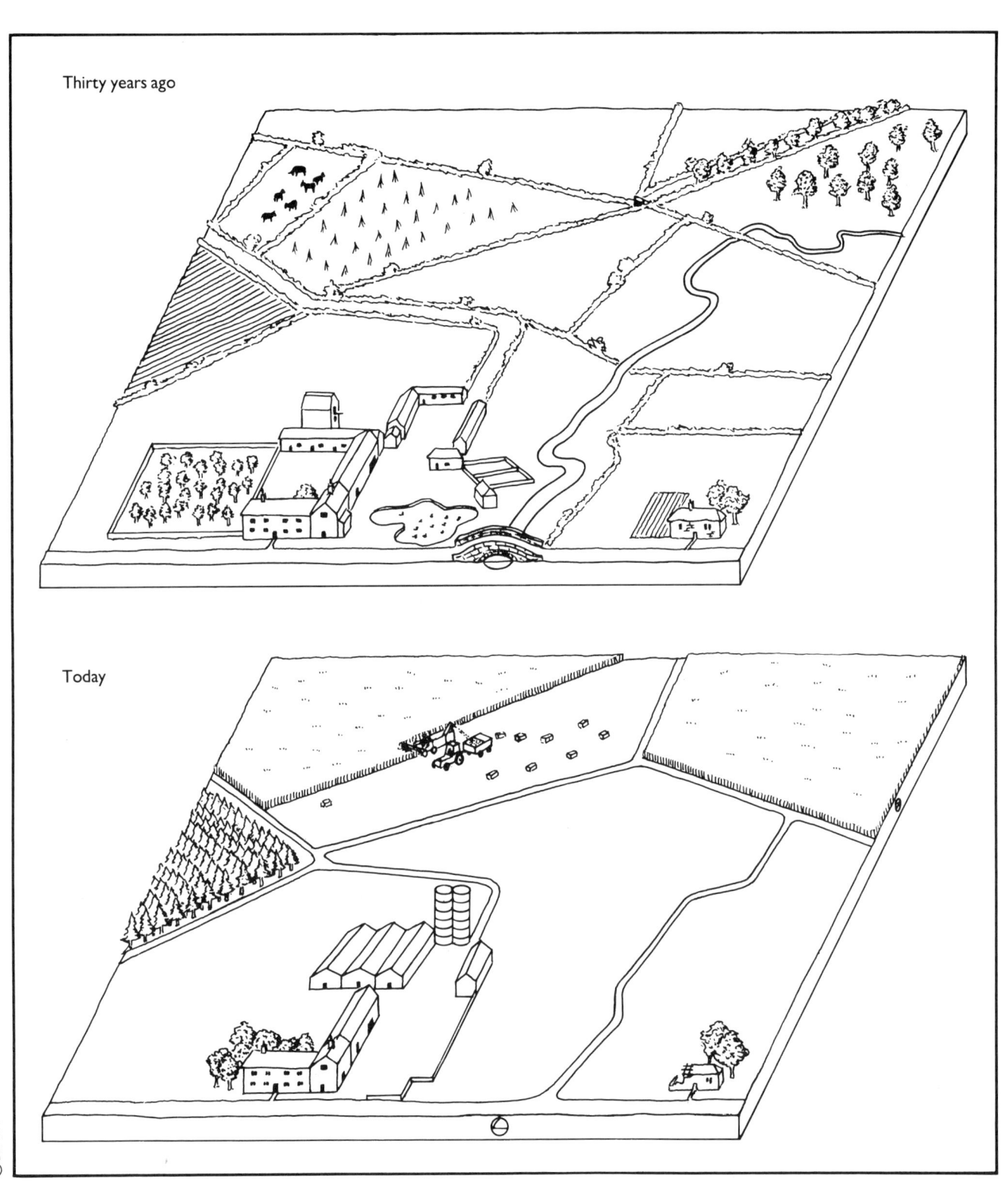

Thirty years ago

Today

©DIAGRAM

Agricultural intensity and land use patterns

City

Market gardening

Arable farming

Dairying

Livestock grazing

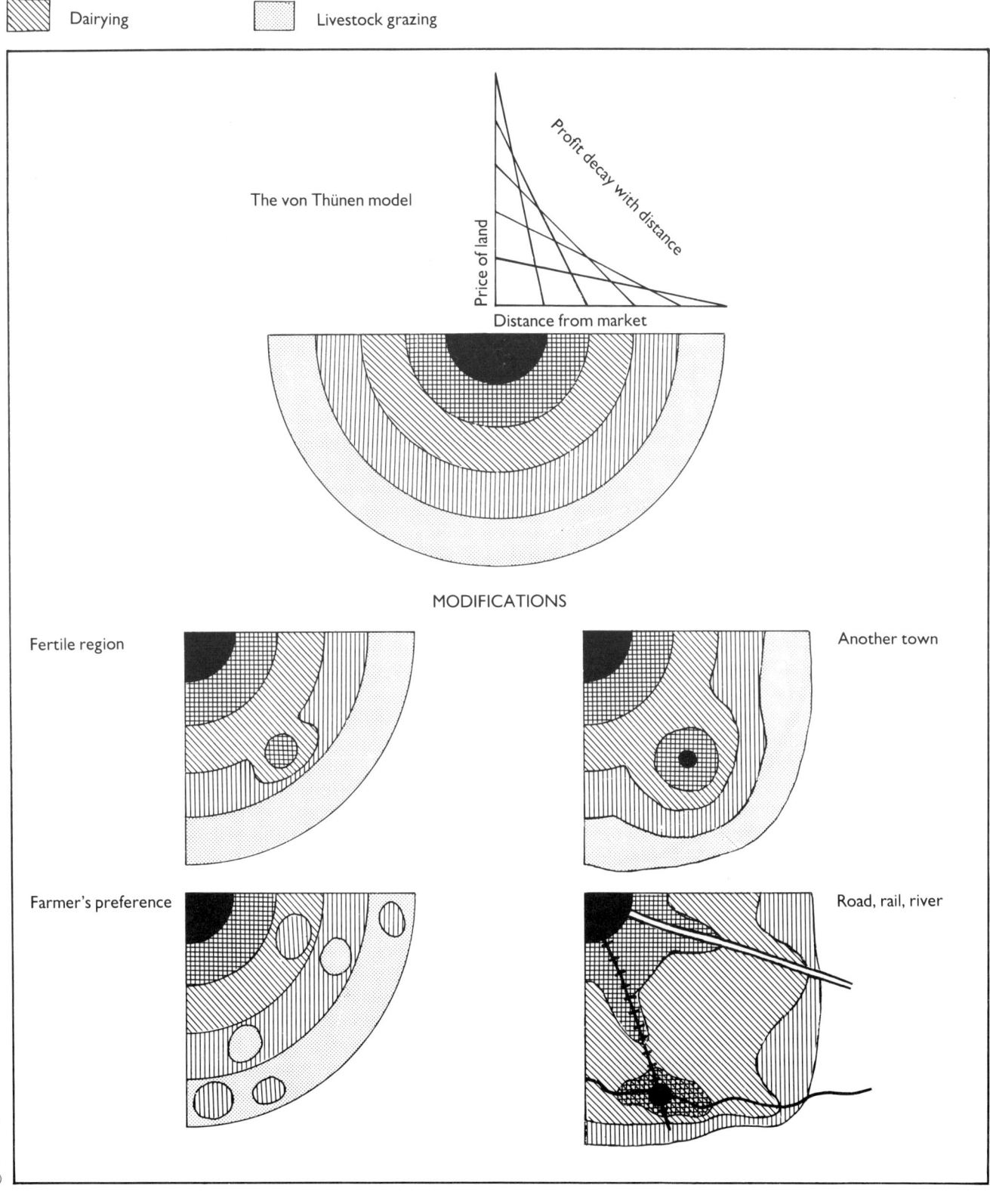

The von Thünen model

Profit decay with distance

Price of land

Distance from market

MODIFICATIONS

Fertile region

Another town

Farmer's preference

Road, rail, river

©DIAGRAM

AGRICULTURE
World fishing: major grounds, catch and methods

Shrimps, prawns, etc.

Herring, anchovy, tuna, etc.

Cod, flat fish, sea bream, etc.

Whales

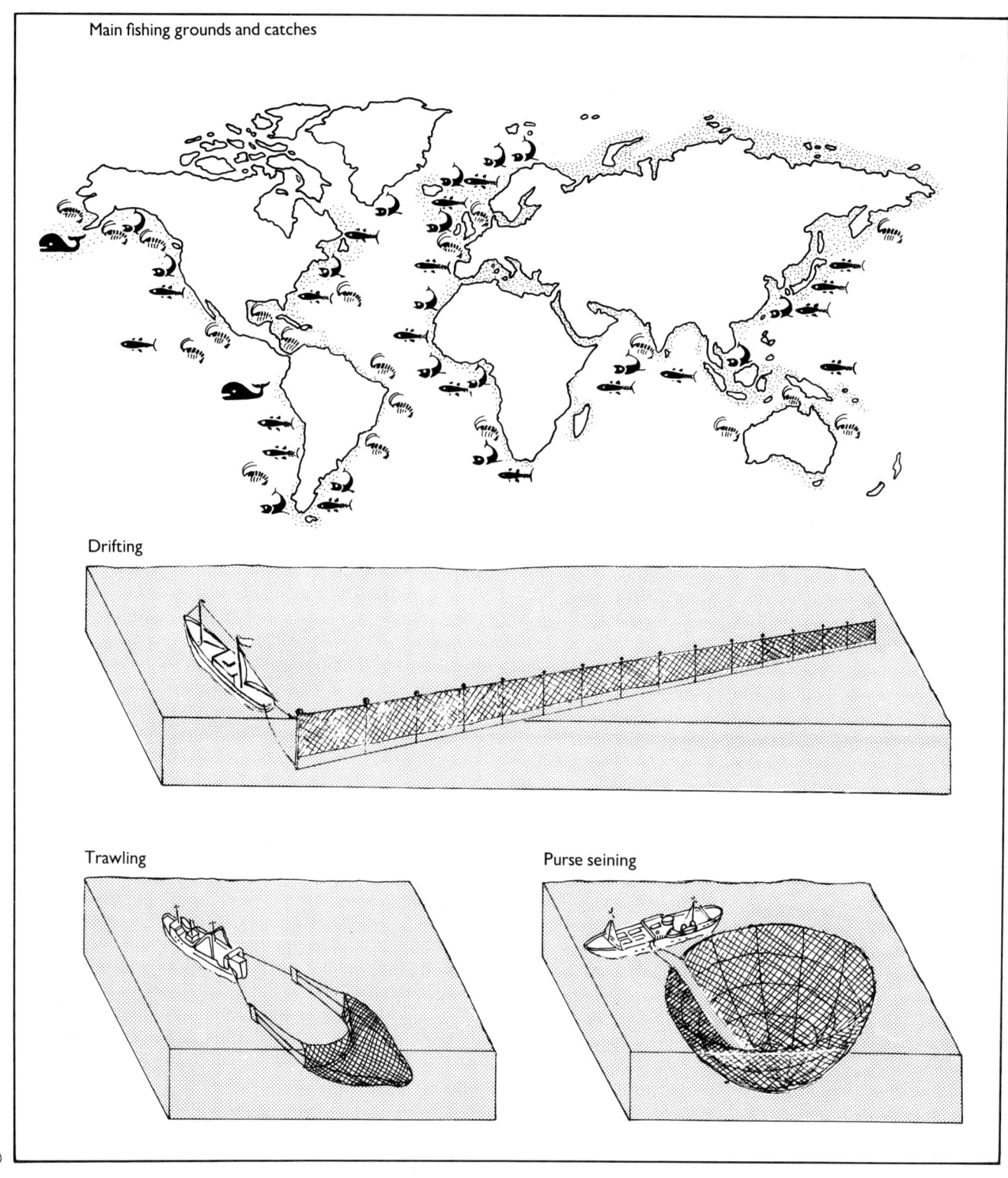

Main fishing grounds and catches

Drifting

Trawling

Purse seining

INDUSTRY
Factors influencing industrial location

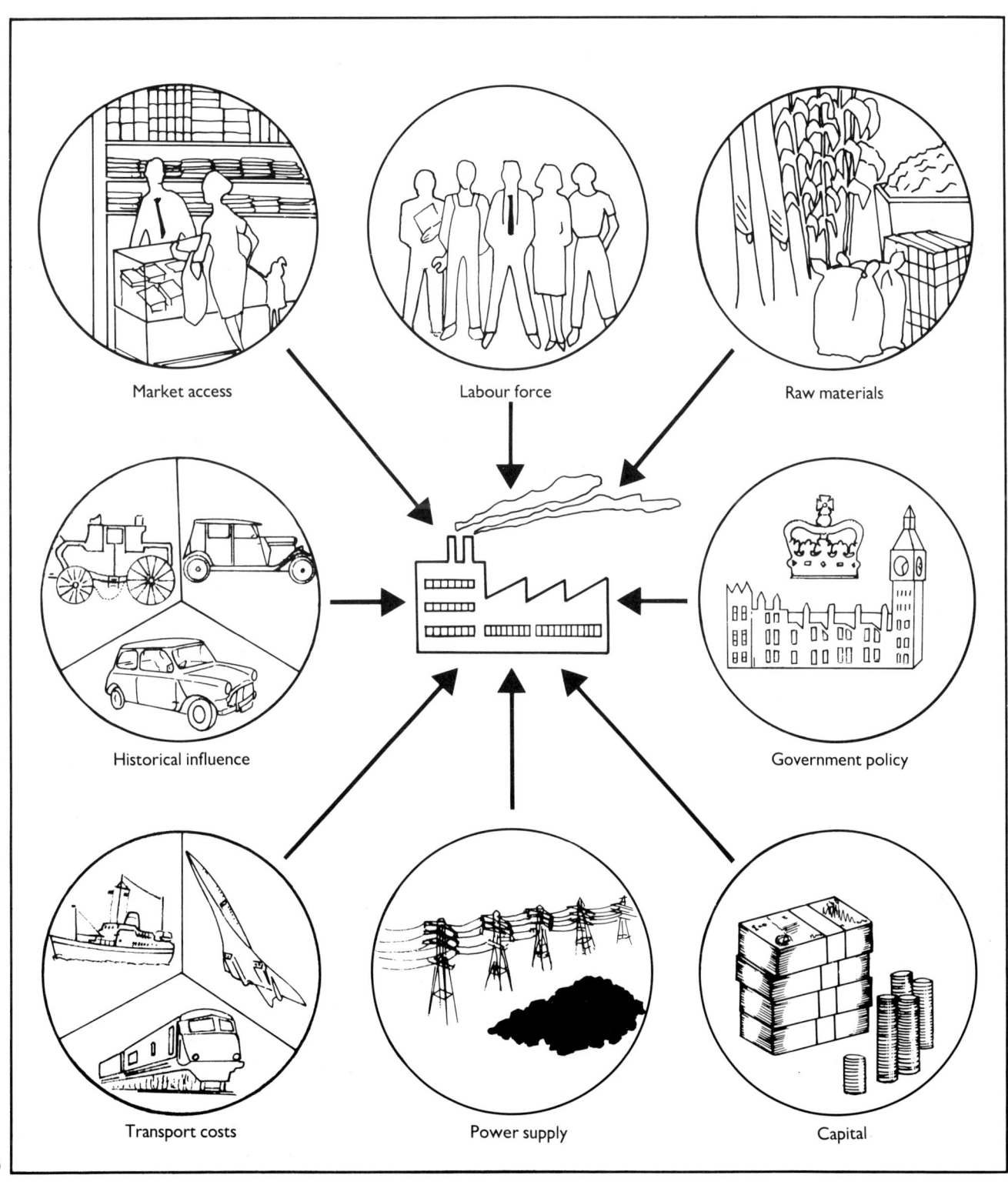

Market access

Labour force

Raw materials

Historical influence

Government policy

Transport costs

Power supply

Capital

©DIAGRAM

INDUSTRY
World manufacturing regions and major sources of industrial raw materials

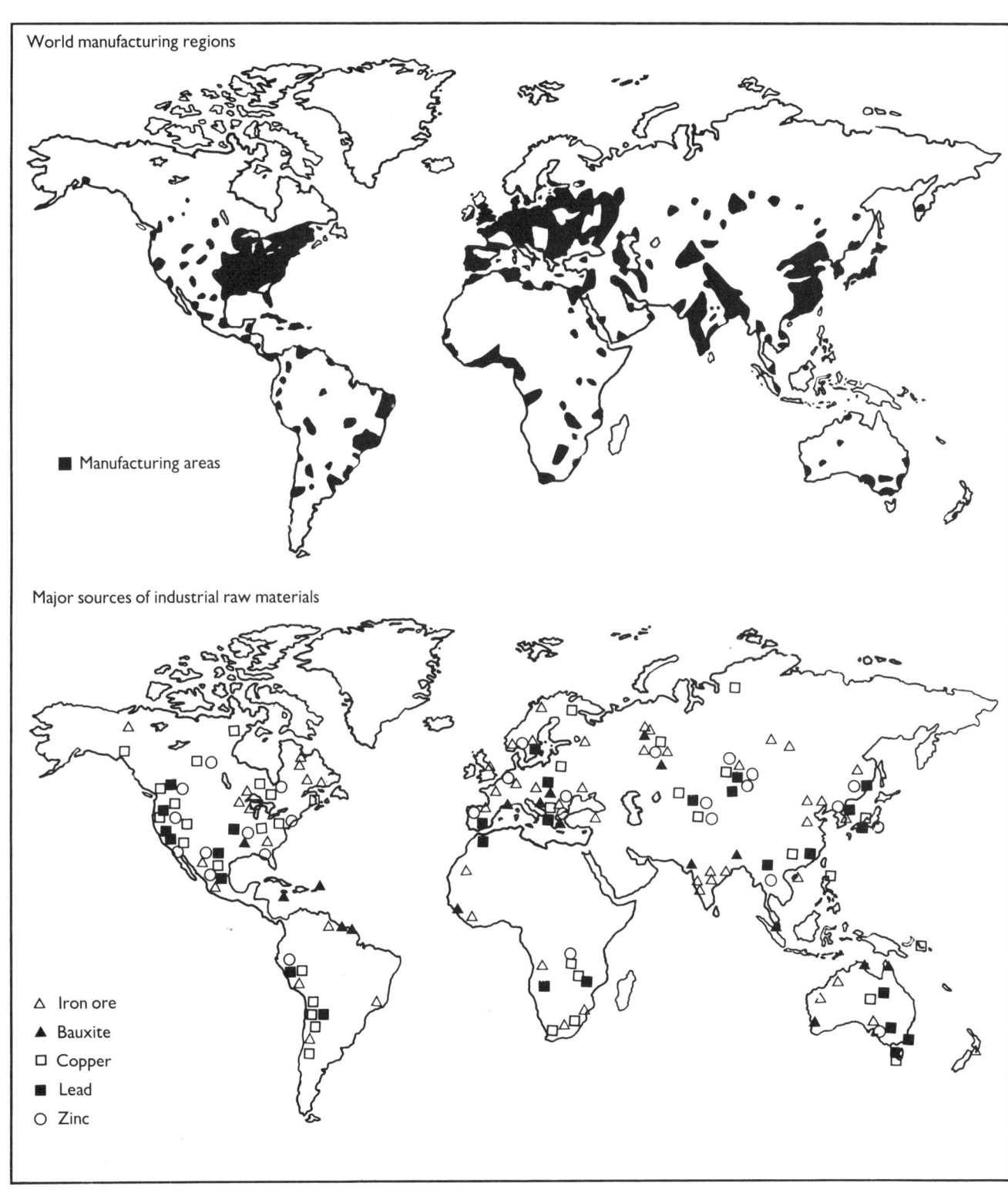

World manufacturing regions

■ Manufacturing areas

Major sources of industrial raw materials

△ Iron ore
▲ Bauxite
□ Copper
■ Lead
○ Zinc

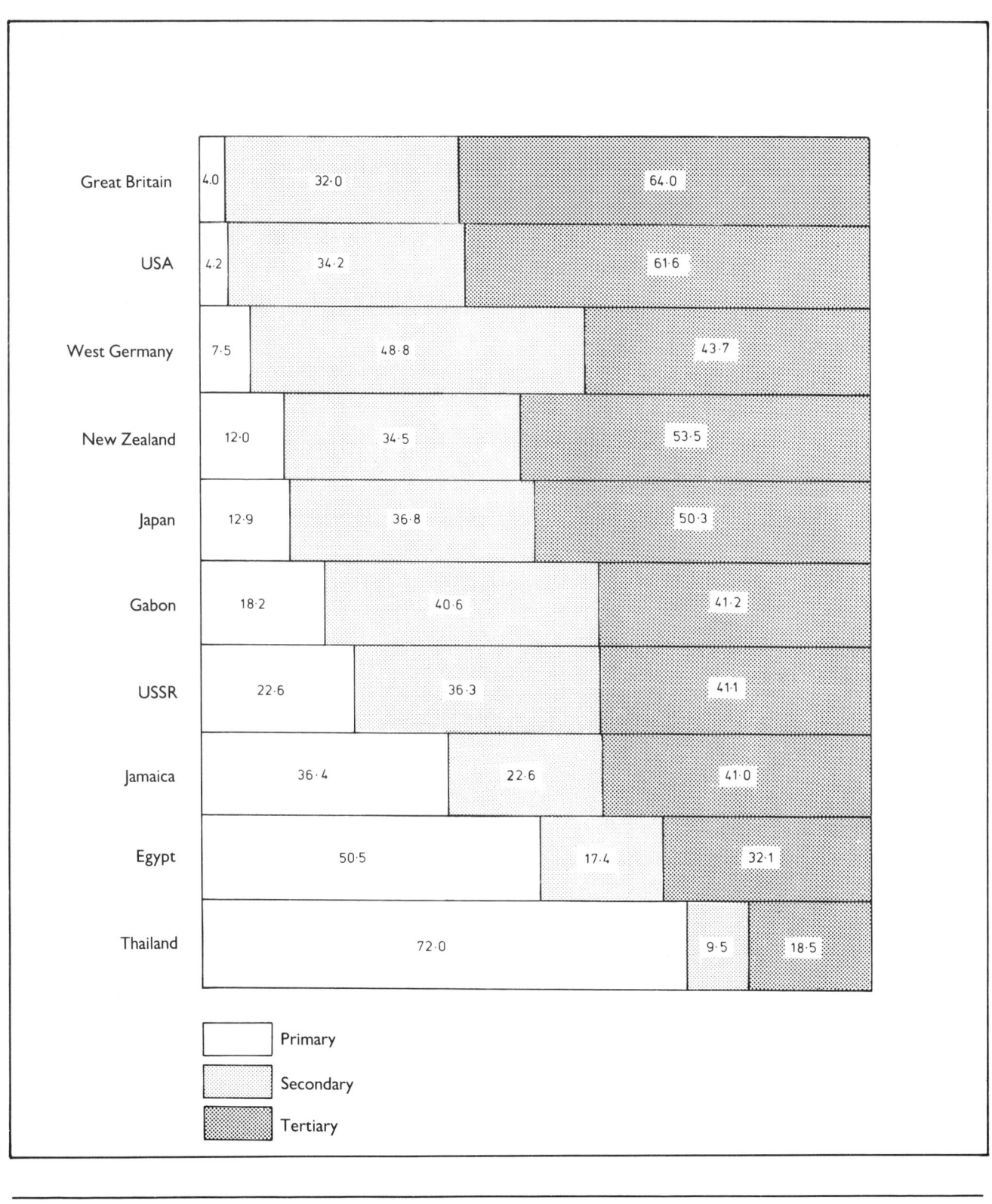

Great Britain: 4.0 | 32·0 | 64·0
USA: 4·2 | 34·2 | 61·6
West Germany: 7·5 | 48·8 | 43·7
New Zealand: 12·0 | 34·5 | 53·5
Japan: 12·9 | 36·8 | 50·3
Gabon: 18·2 | 40·6 | 41·2
USSR: 22·6 | 36·3 | 41·1
Jamaica: 36·4 | 22·6 | 41·0
Egypt: 50·5 | 17·4 | 32·1
Thailand: 72·0 | 9·5 | 18·5

Primary
Secondary
Tertiary

INDUSTRY
Primary industry: a modern coalmine

1 Personnel winding tower
2 Baths and canteen
3 Repair workshop
4 Delivery trucks
5 Extractor fan

6 Coal shaft winding tower
7 Rail loading bay
8 Coke and coal gas plant
9 Gas storage tanks
10 Roof supports

11 Conveyor belt
12 Mining machine (longwall)
13 Unexploited coal seam
14 Mining machine (continuous)
15 Outgoing ventilation shaft

16 Sump
17 Incoming ventilation shaft

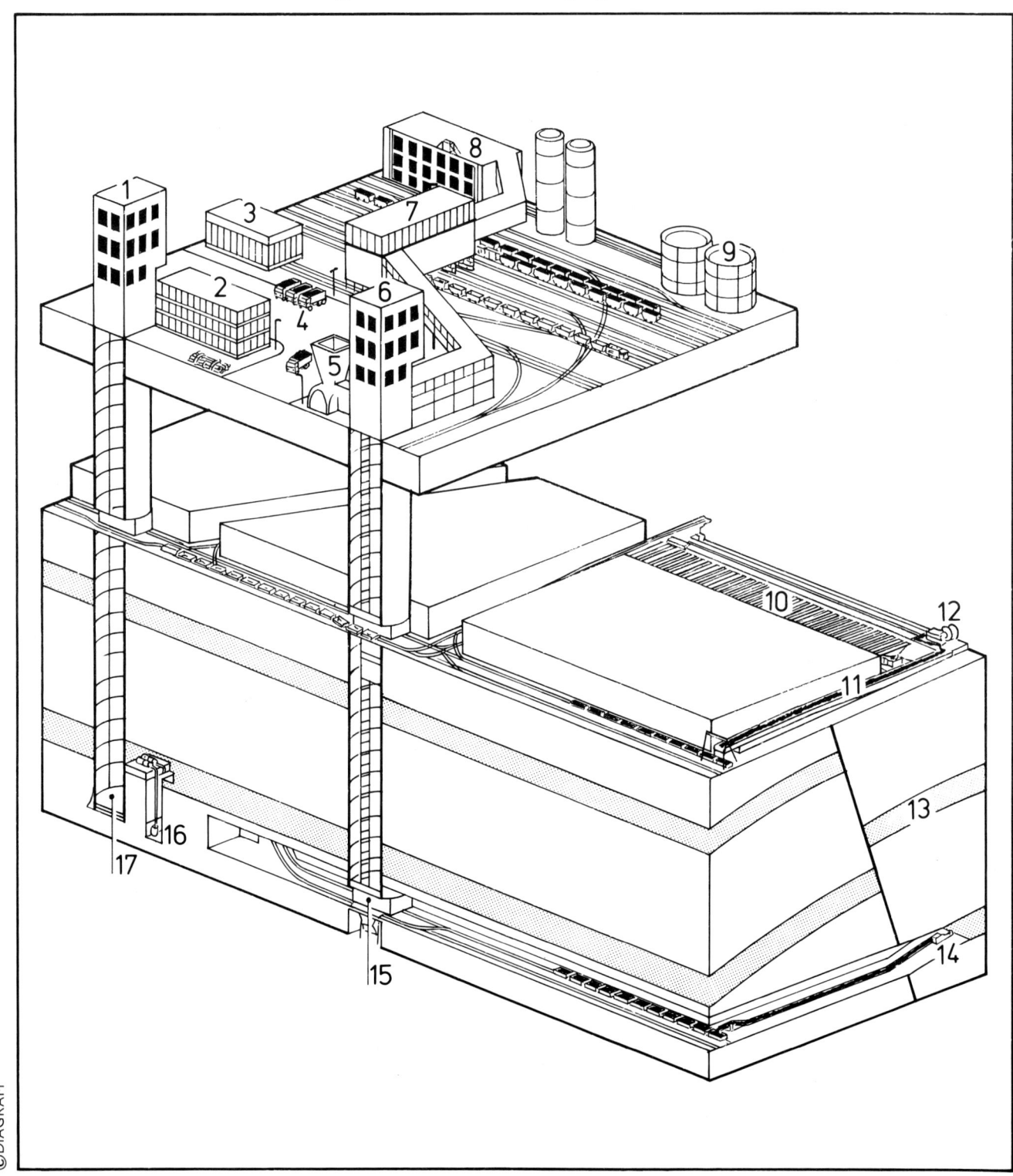

INDUSTRY
Heavy manufacturing: iron and steel making

1 Limestone quarry
2 Coking coal mine
3 Iron ore
4 Sintering plant
5 Blast furnace

6 Slag removal
7 Molten iron for direct casting
8 Mixing with scrap steel
9 Melting
10 Treating with oxygen

11 Treating with limestone
12 Molten steel running off
13 Detritus removal
14 Steel for casting
15 Ingots

16 Bar rolling
17 Sheet rolling
18 Steel forging

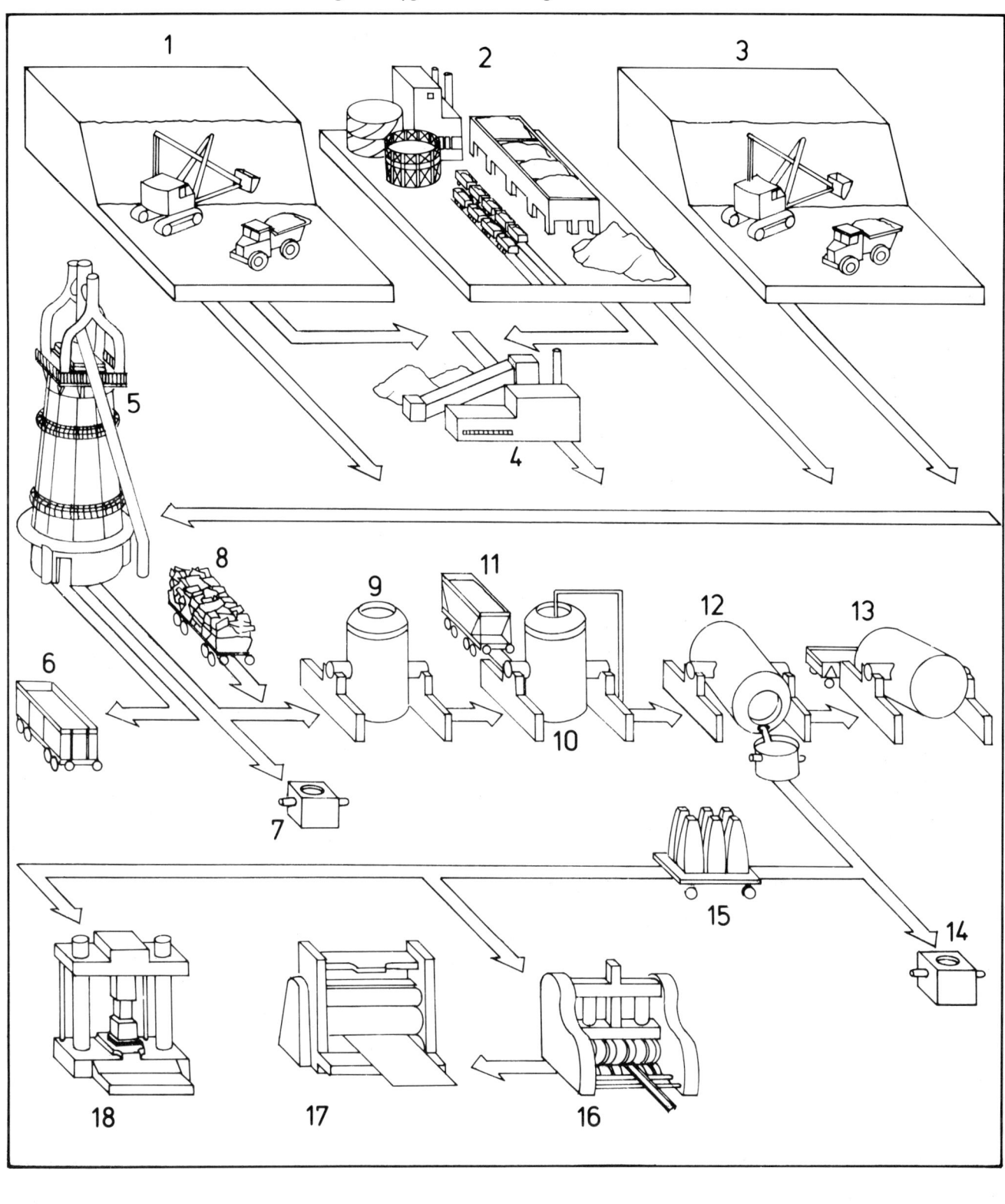

©DIAGRAM

Assembly industry: car production

<u>Sequence of operations</u>

1 Body pressing	**6** Base primer dipping	**11** Dashboard installing	**16** Washing
2 Underbody and front joining	**7** Primer spraying	**12** Seat fitting	**17** Valet service
3 Adding sides	**8** Paint spraying	**13** Engine and tank fitting	**18** Driving away
4 Adding roof	**9** Under wing waxing	**14** Wheel fitting	
5 Adding doors and bonnet	**10** Removing doors, adding glass	**15** Roller testing	

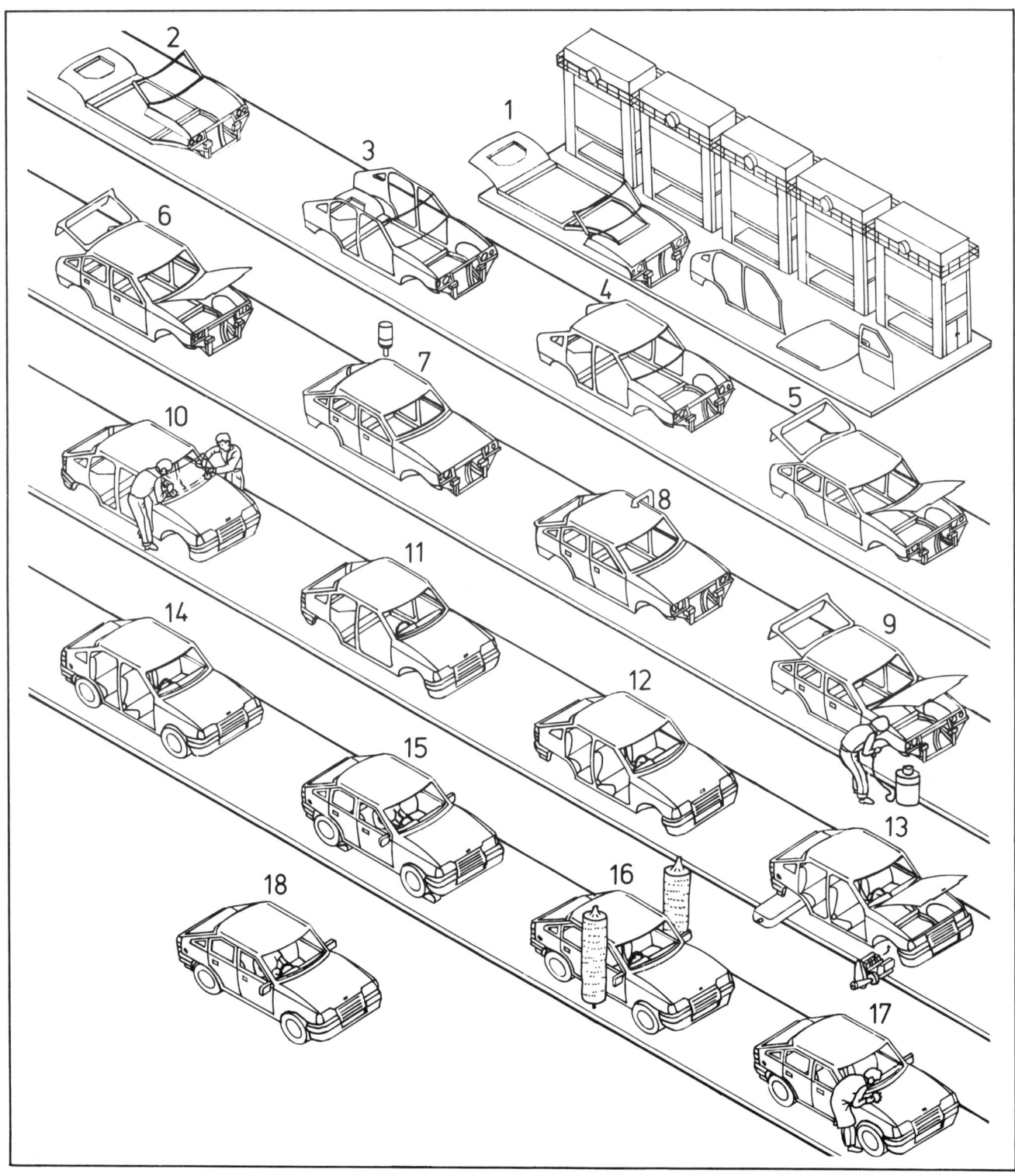

©DIAGRAM

INDUSTRY
A major enclosed shopping centre: Brent Cross in North London

1 Department stores
2 Supermarket
3 Two-storey stores
4 Public areas

 Individual shops

 Services, banks

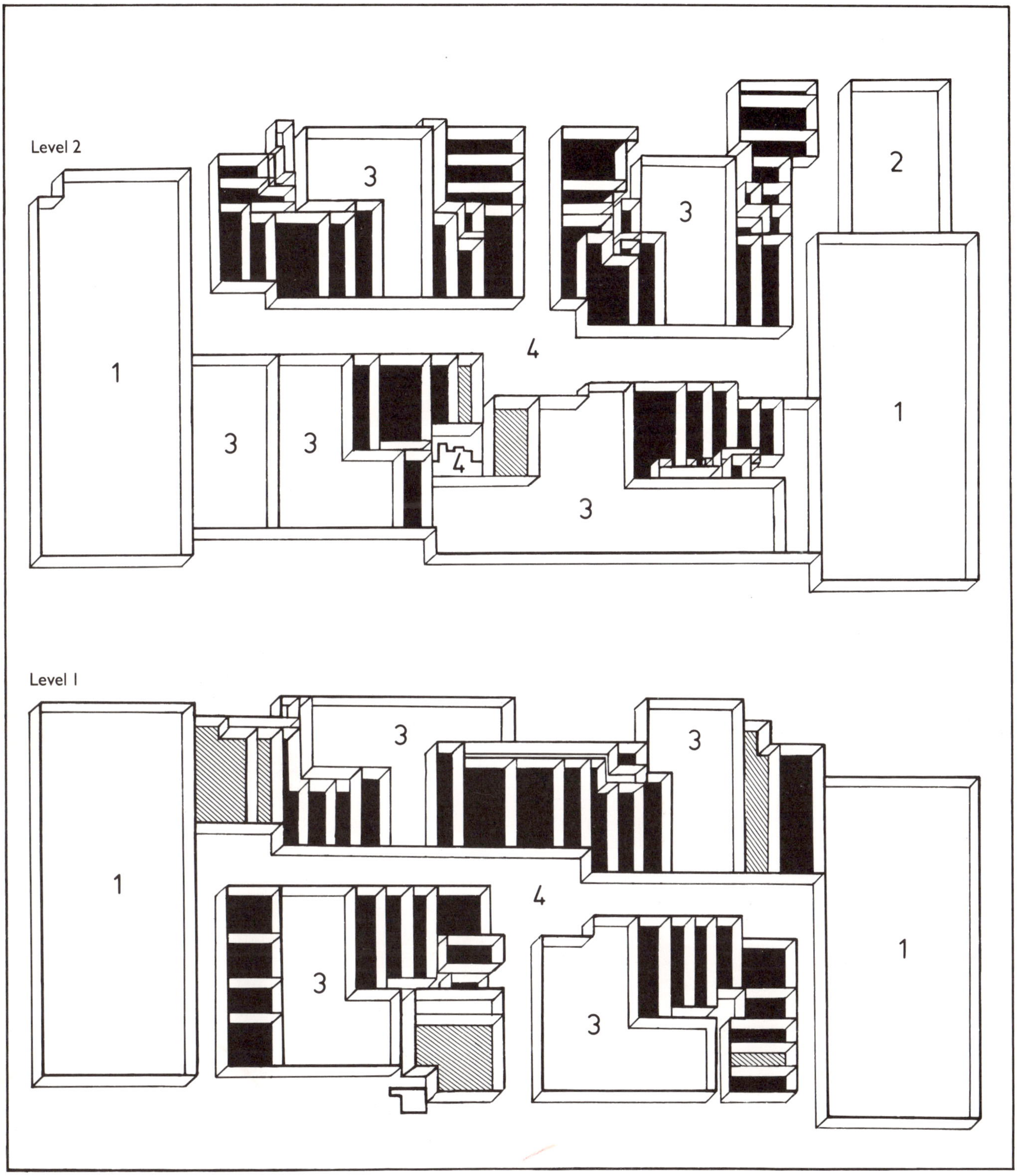

Level 2

Level 1

©DIAGRAM

ENERGY
World energy budget

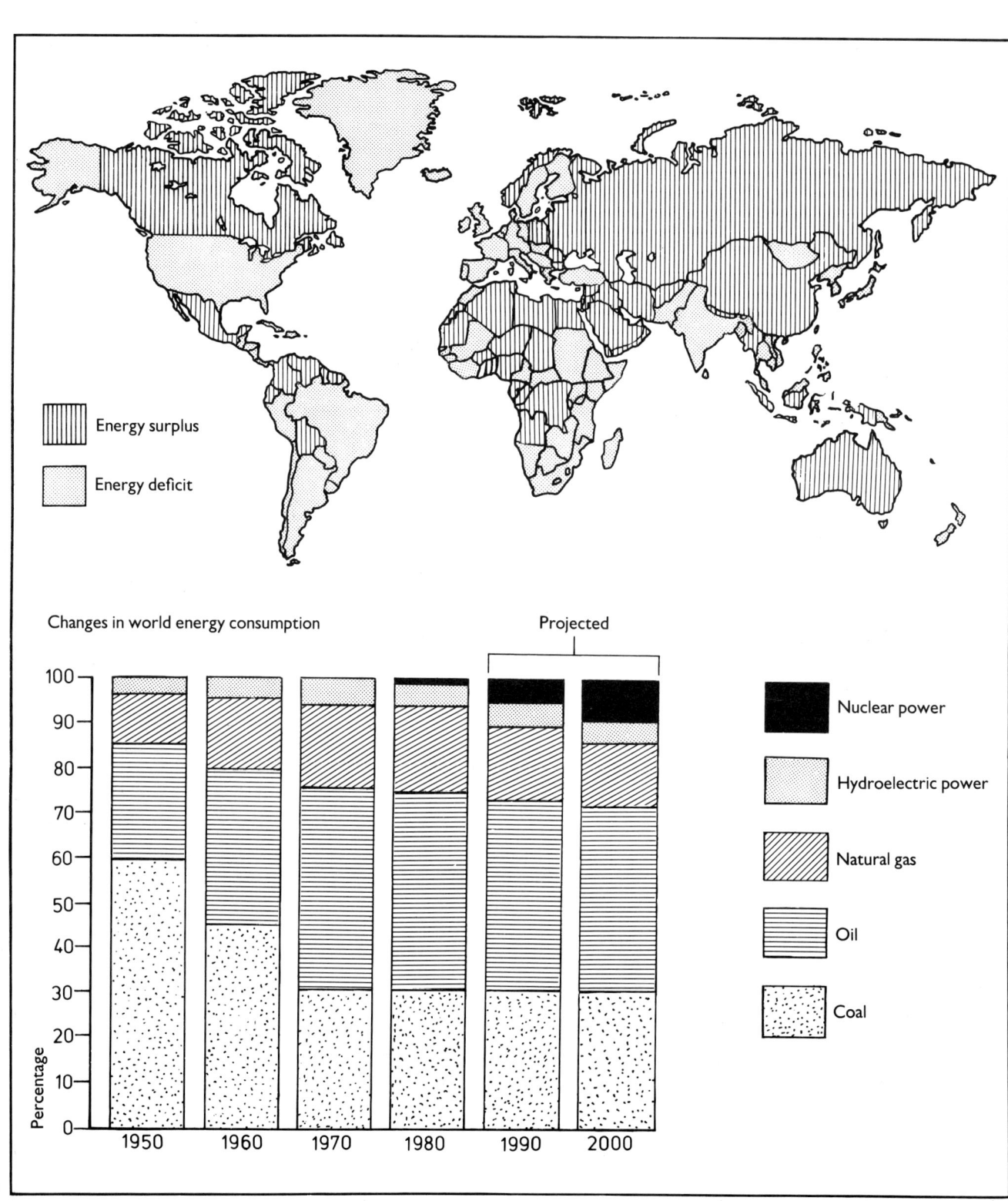

Energy surplus

Energy deficit

Changes in world energy consumption

Projected

Nuclear power

Hydroelectric power

Natural gas

Oil

Coal

Percentage

©DIAGRAM

Hydro-electric power production

Pumped storage system

1 Reservoir	**6** Generator
2 Sluices	**7** Pumps
3 Dam	**8** Water outlets
4 Control building	**9** Water inlets
5 Turbine	**10** Stilling pool

© DIAGRAM

ENERGY
Nuclear power station

1 Cooling towers
2 Cool water
3 Steam generator
4 Cool helium
5 Reactor core
6 Hot helium
7 Turbine
8 Generator
9 Cool steam
10 Output transformer
11 Power lines to grid system

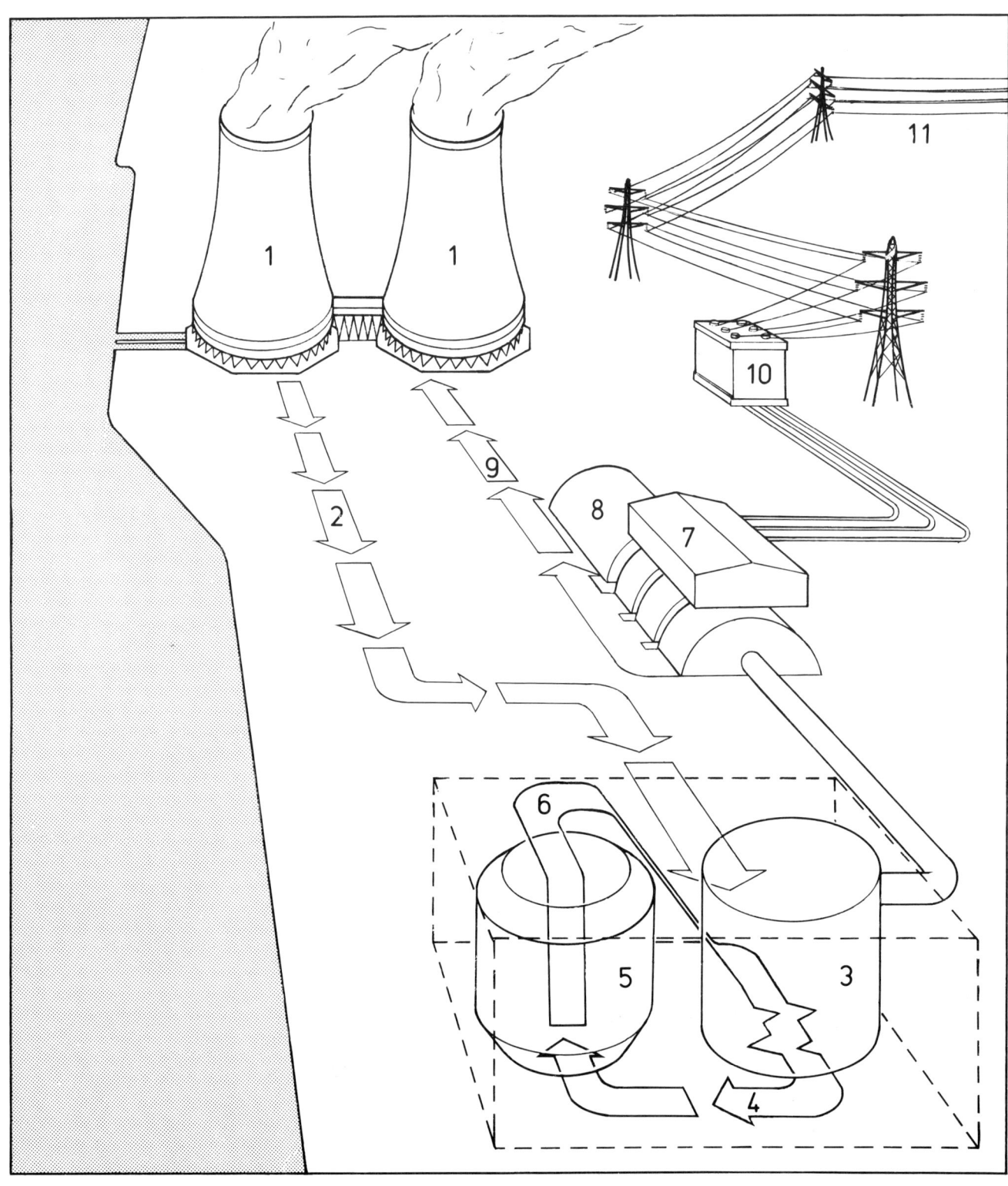

ENERGY
Oil and gas exploration and production

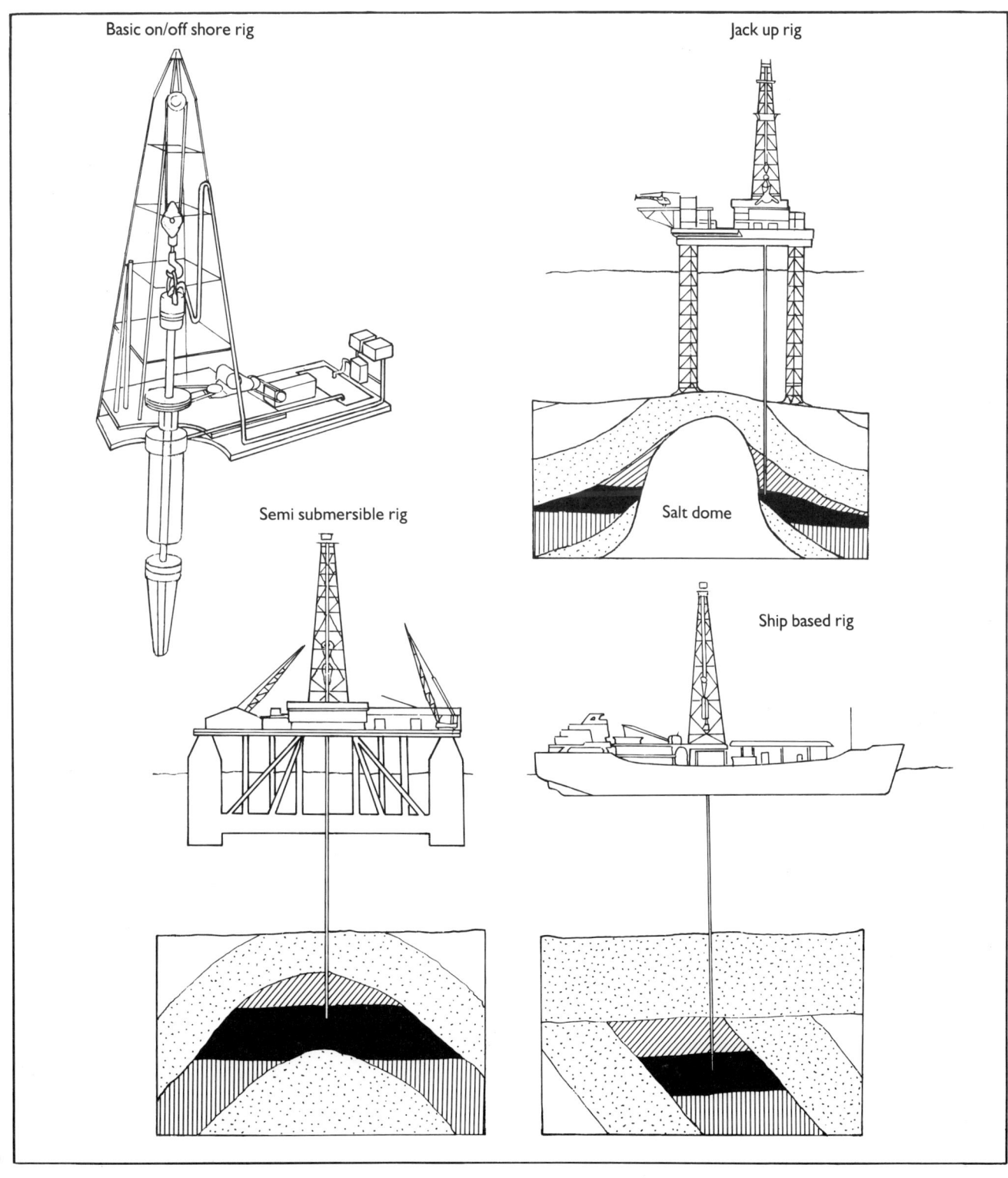

Gas

Oil

Impermeable rock

Water-bearing rock

Basic on/off shore rig

Jack up rig

Salt dome

Semi submersible rig

Ship based rig

©DIAGRAM

Alternative energy sources:
solar, wind, tidal and wave

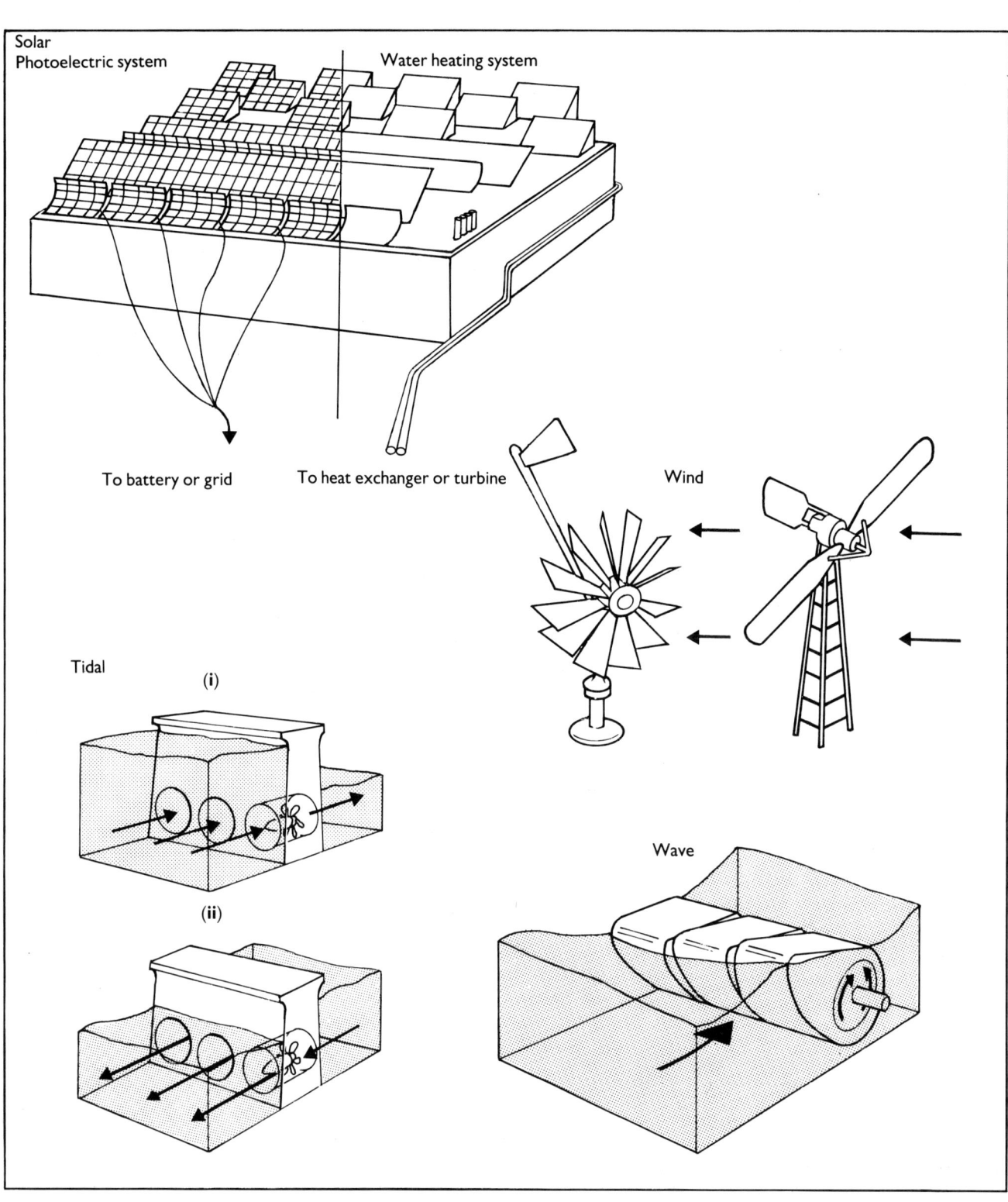

Solar
Photoelectric system

Water heating system

To battery or grid

To heat exchanger or turbine

Wind

Tidal

(i)

(ii)

Wave

TRANSPORT
Properties of networks

Increasing network complexity linking six locations

Alternative networks linking five settlements

Comparison of transport types

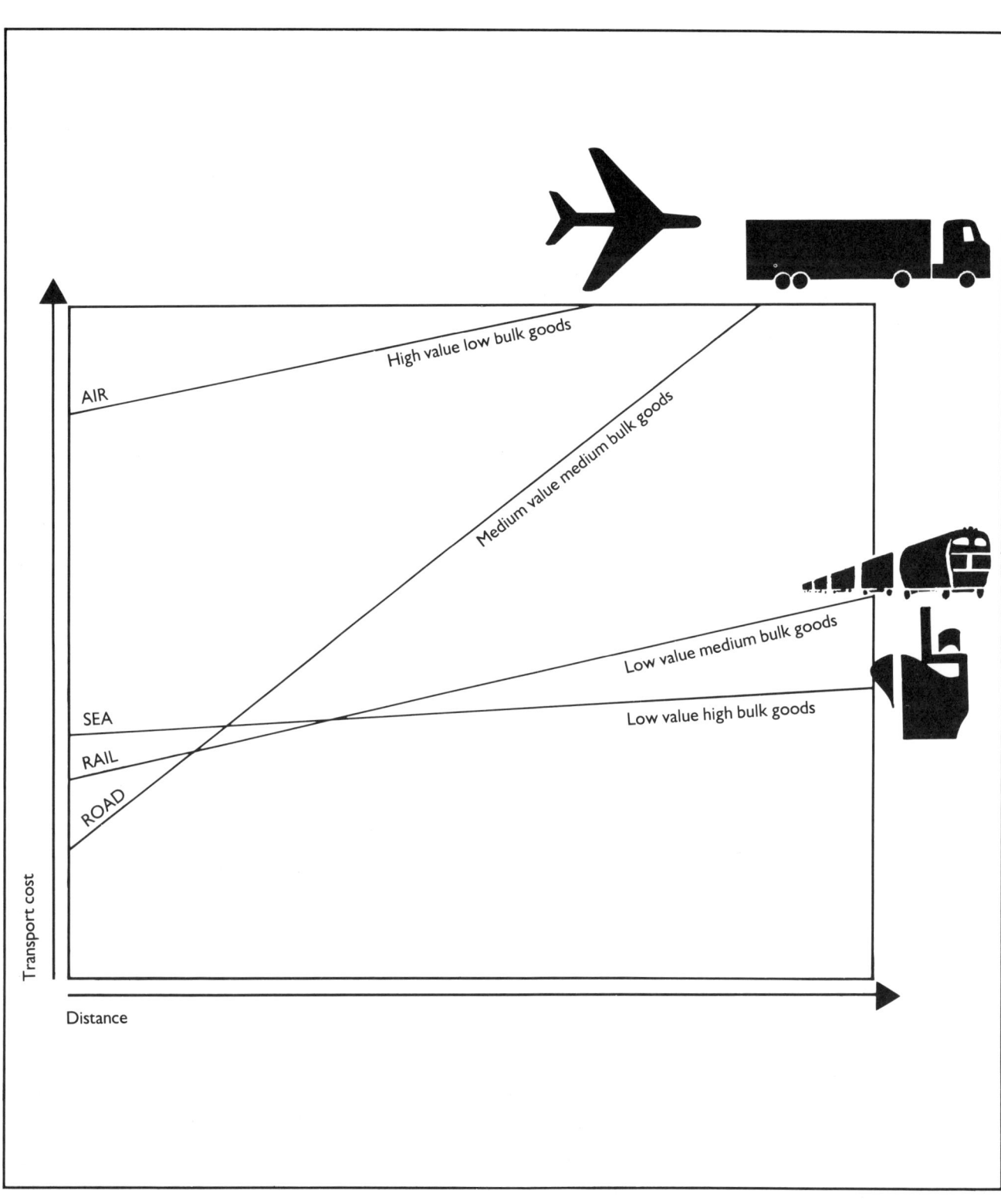

High value low bulk goods

AIR

Medium value medium bulk goods

Low value medium bulk goods

SEA

RAIL

Low value high bulk goods

ROAD

Transport cost

Distance

TRANSPORT
Isochrones: comparison of distance with travel time

Based on rail travel times 1986

Hours

7

6

5

4

3

2

Aberdeen

Perth

Dundee

Edinburgh

Glasgow

Carlisle

Newcastle

Hull

Blackpool

Bradford

Sheffield

York

Manchester

Preston

Liverpool

Nottingham

Norwich

Crewe

Cambridge

Leicester

Birmingham

Peterborough

Ipswich

Swansea

Cardiff

Oxford

London

Bristol

Southampton

Dover

Exeter

Bournemouth

Plymouth

Brighton

Torquay

Penzance

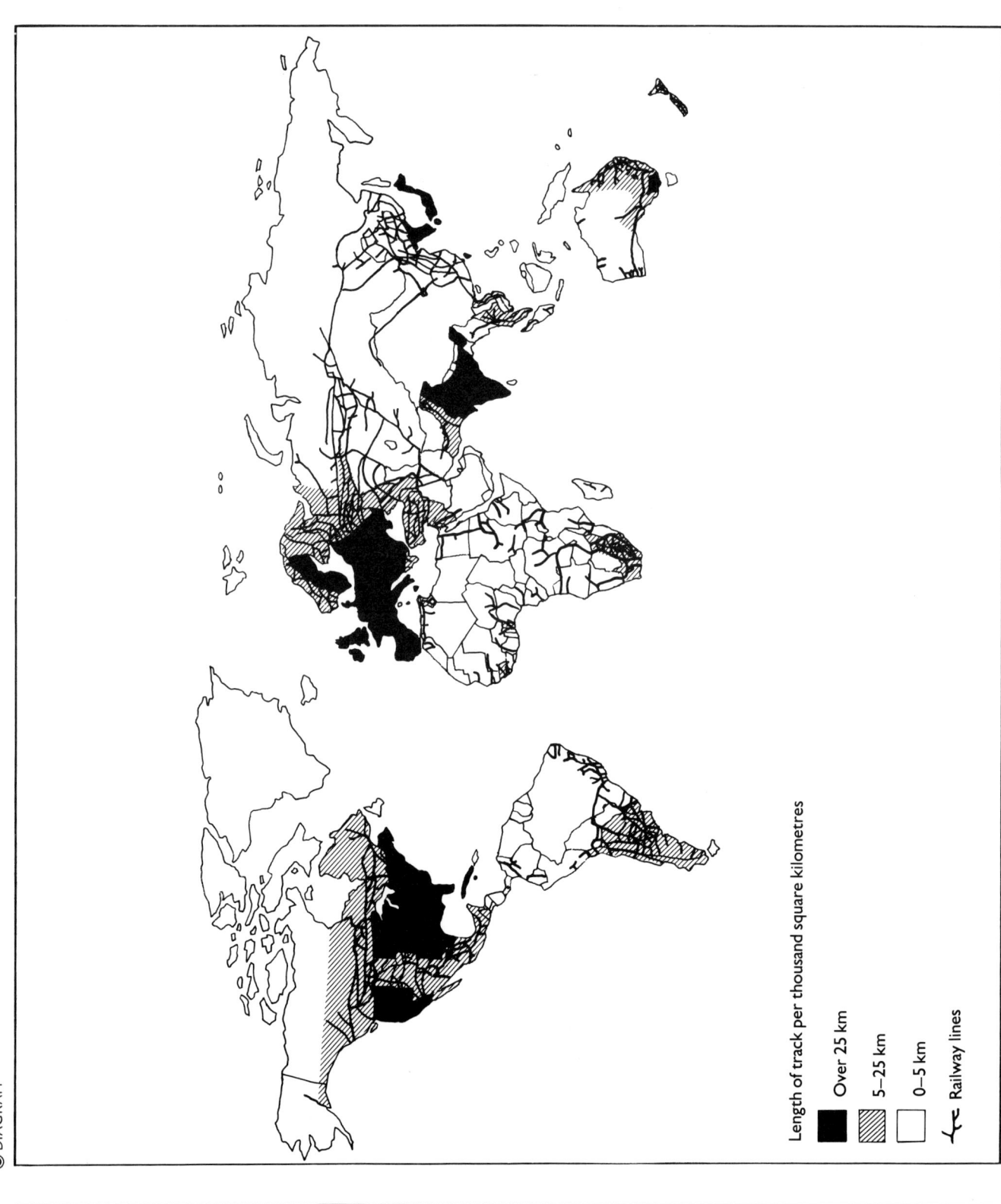

Length of track per thousand square kilometres

Over 25 km

5–25 km

0–5 km

Railway lines

TRANSPORT
Sequence of port development

Urban area

Sea

Airport

Road

Railway

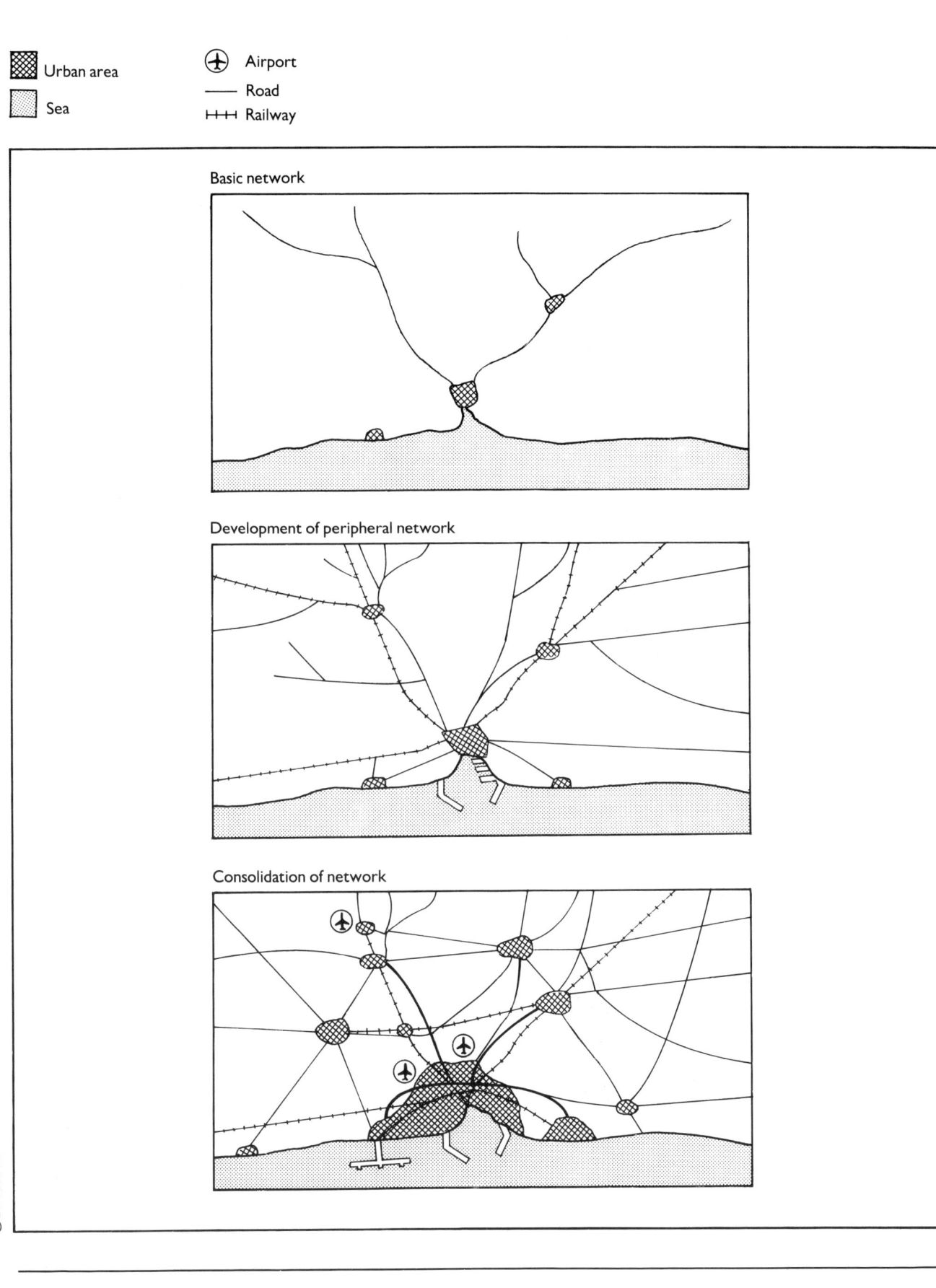

Basic network

Development of peripheral network

Consolidation of network

©DIAGRAM

TRANSPORT
A modern airport

1 Plane exhaust gases
2 Passenger traffic to and from airport
3 Freight vehicles serving airport
4 Reception interference

5 Noise and vibration
6 Emergency units
7 Aircraft arrivals
8 Aircraft departures
9 Weather station

10 Aircraft refuelling
11 Medical centre
12 Observation decks
13 Check-in
14 Control tower

15 Shops and restaurants
16 Passport control
17 Customs and police

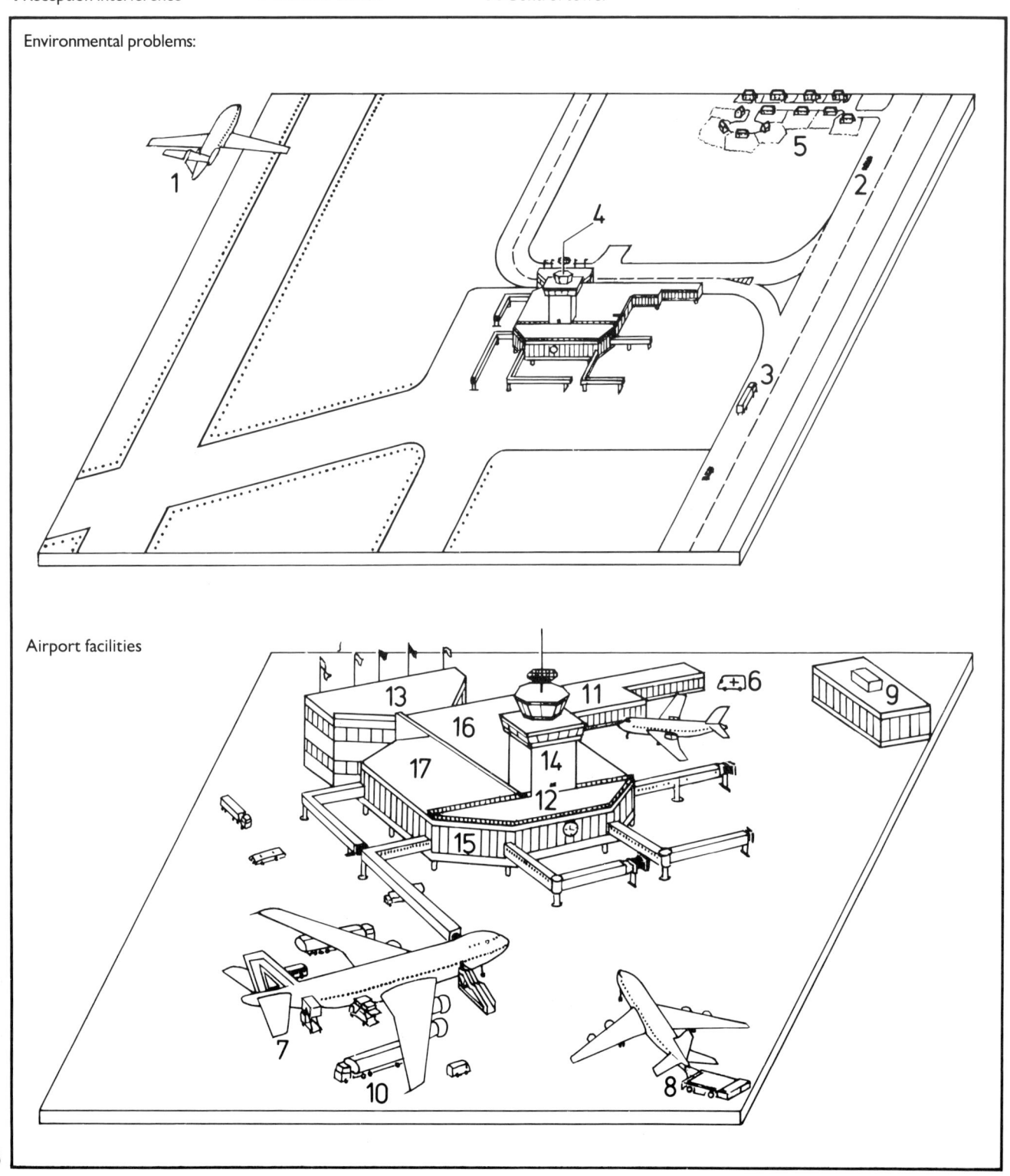

Environmental problems:

Airport facilities

©DIAGRAM

_____

_____

_____

_____

_____

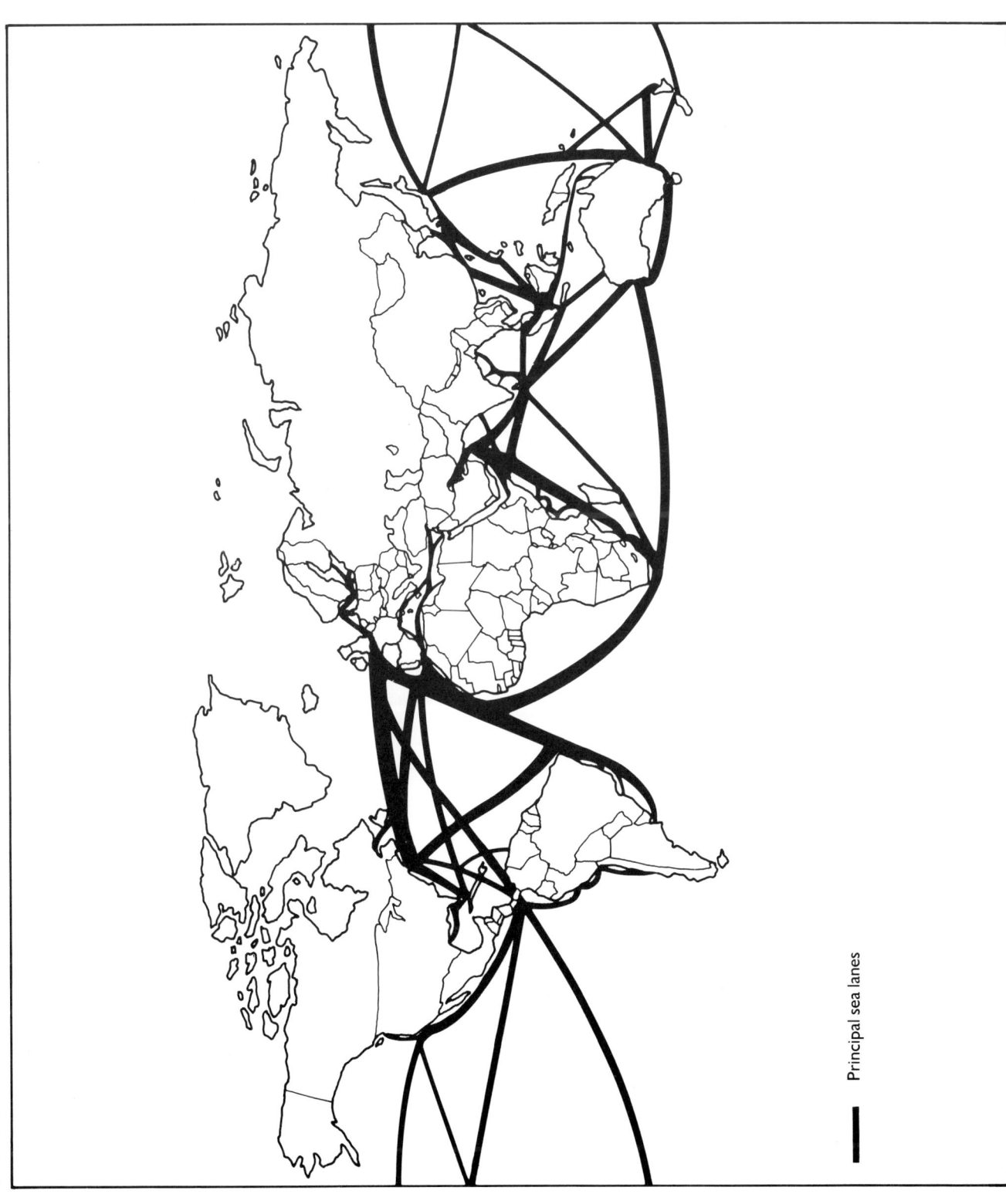

Principal sea lanes

© DIAGRAM

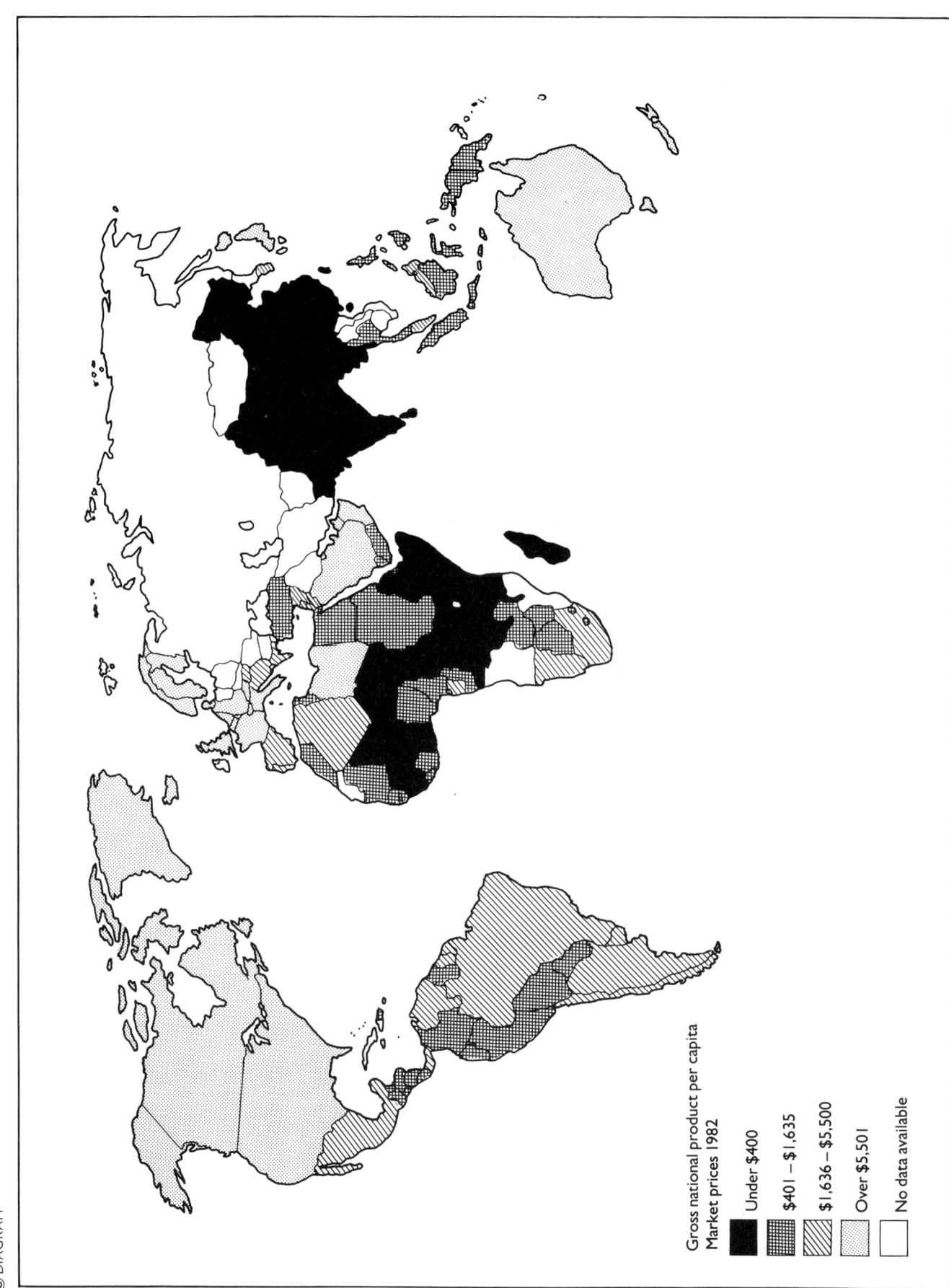

Gross national product per capita
Market prices 1982

- Under $400
- $401 – $1,635
- $1,636 – $5,500
- Over $5,501
- No data available

ECONOMIC DEVELOPMENT
International aid: major donor countries and recipients

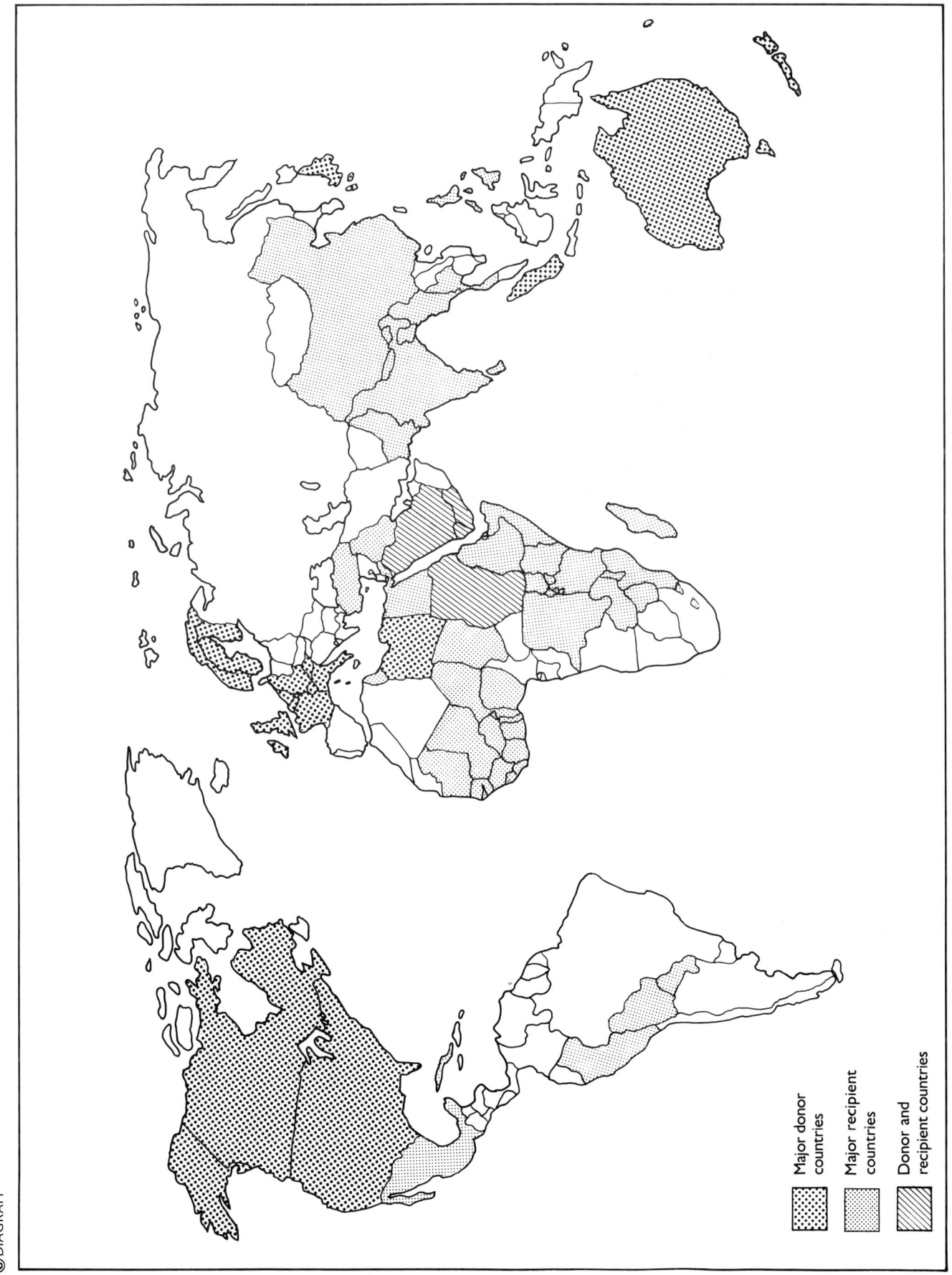

Major donor
countries

Major recipient
countries

Donor and
recipient countries

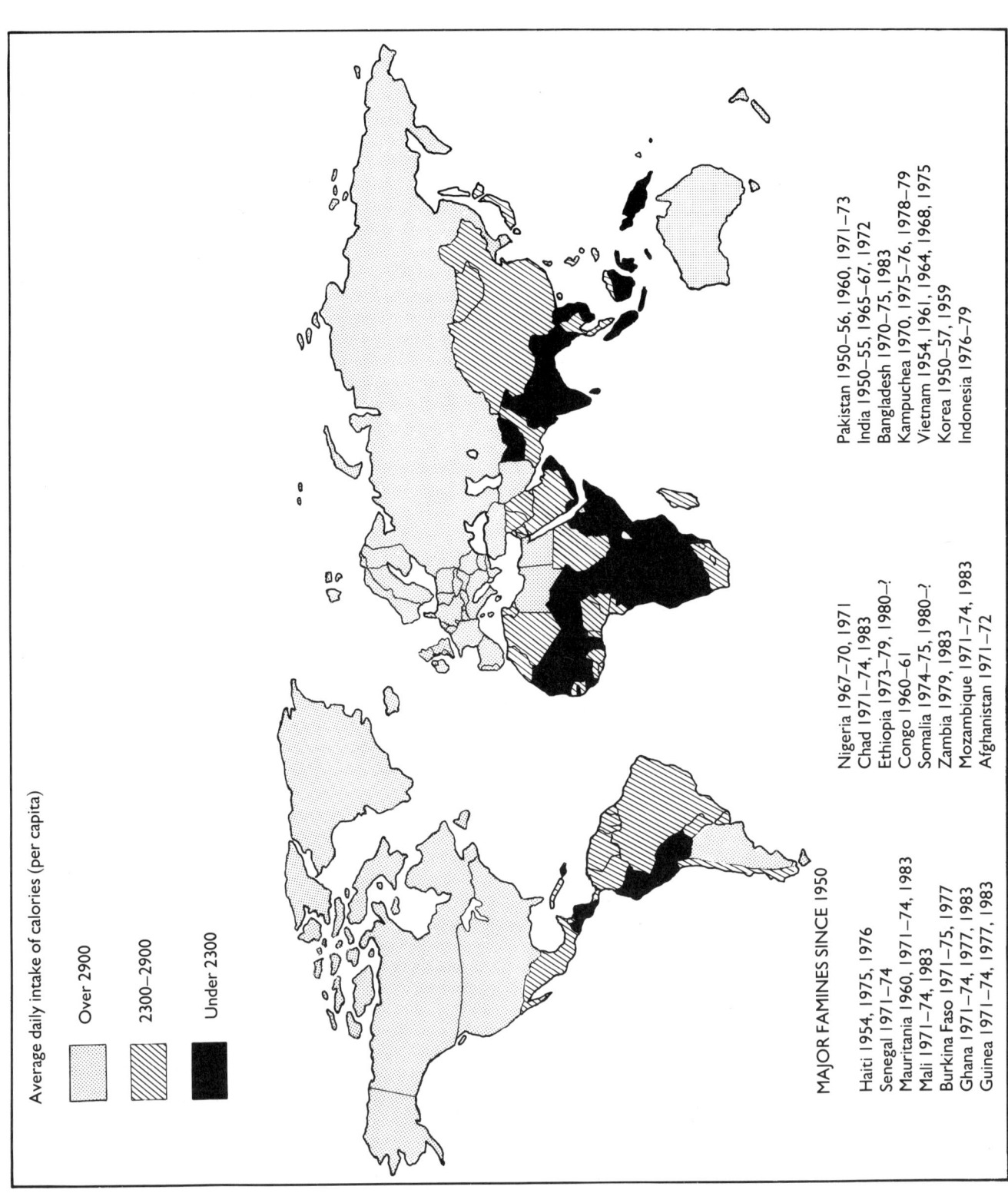

Average daily intake of calories (per capita)

Over 2900

2300–2900

Under 2300

MAJOR FAMINES SINCE 1950

Haiti 1954, 1975, 1976
Senegal 1971–74
Mauritania 1960, 1971–74, 1983
Mali 1971–74, 1983
Burkina Faso 1971–75, 1977
Ghana 1971–74, 1977, 1983
Guinea 1971–74, 1977, 1983

Nigeria 1967–70, 1971
Chad 1971–74, 1983
Ethiopia 1973–79, 1980–?
Congo 1960–61
Somalia 1974–75, 1980–?
Zambia 1979, 1983
Mozambique 1971–74, 1983
Afghanistan 1971–72

Pakistan 1950–56, 1960, 1971–73
India 1950–55, 1965–67, 1972
Bangladesh 1970–75, 1983
Kampuchea 1970, 1975–76, 1978–79
Vietnam 1954, 1961, 1964, 1968, 1975
Korea 1950–57, 1959
Indonesia 1976–79

© DIAGRAM

ECONOMIC DEVELOPMENT
Types of government

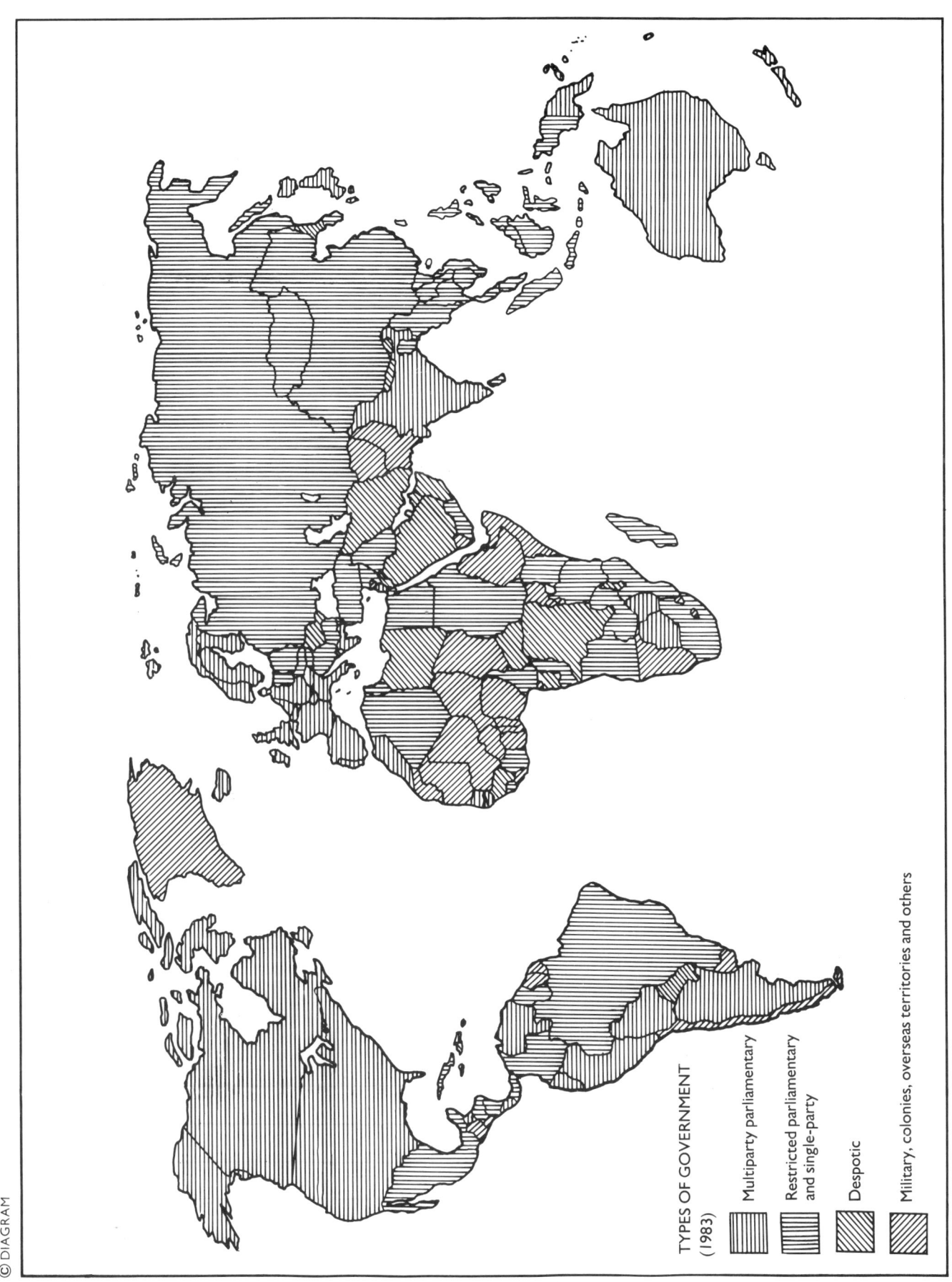

TYPES OF GOVERNMENT
(1983)

Multiparty parliamentary

Restricted parliamentary
and single-party

Despotic

Military, colonies, overseas territories and others

ENVIRONMENT
Urban expansion

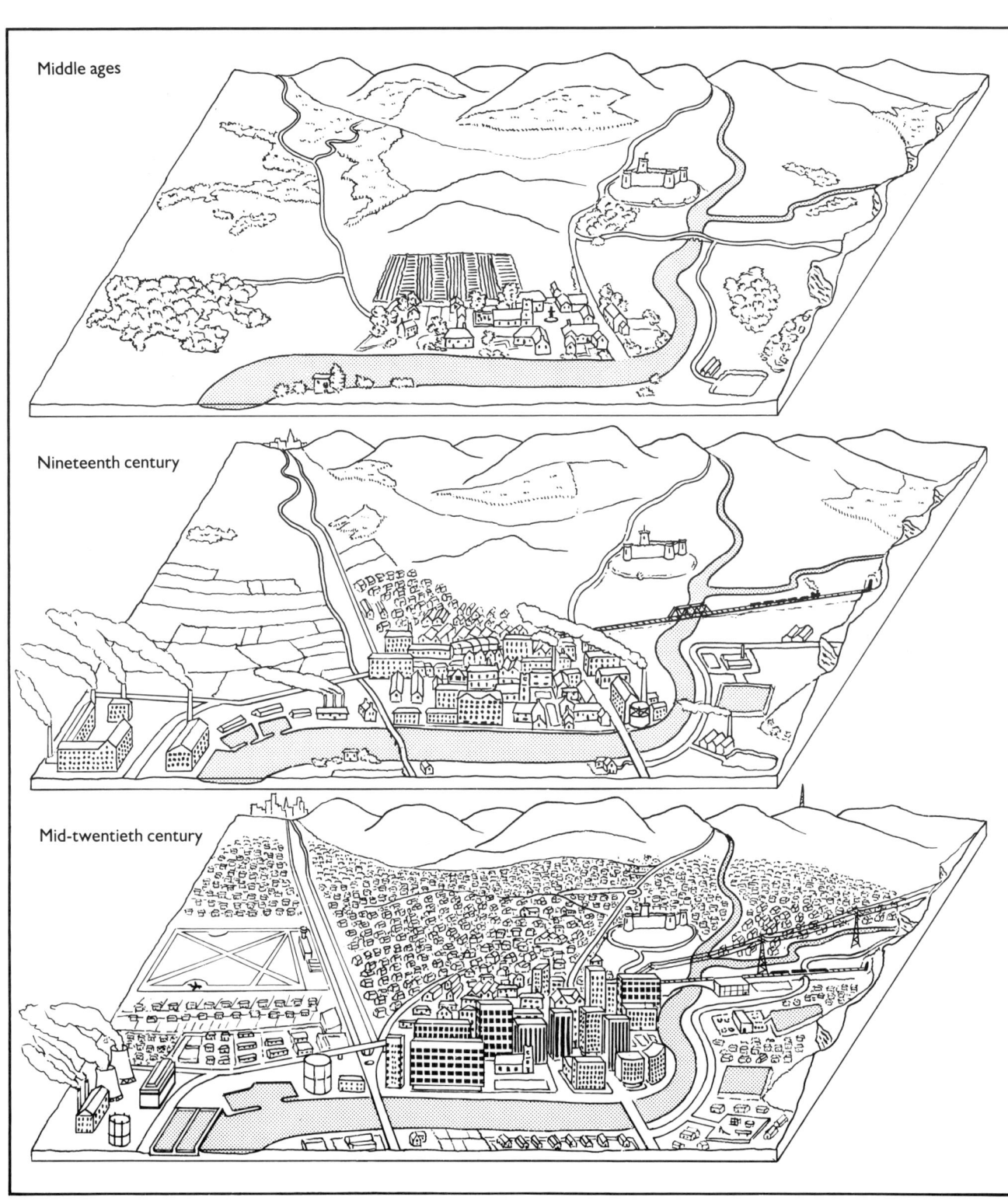

Middle ages

Nineteenth century

Mid-twentieth century

ENVIRONMENT
Land use conflicts

1 Mountaineering
2 Hillwalking
3 Quarrying
4 Reservoirs
5 Power stations

6 Cable cars
7 Motorways
8 Fishing
9 Wild life nature trails
10 Yachting and watersports

11 Industry using water
12 Settlements
13 Sewage disposal
14 Harbour
15 River transport

16 Farming

ENVIRONMENT
Conflicts on the coastline

1 Coastguard station
2 Cliff erosion
3 Farming
4 Industry using water
5 Ship building
6 Port facilities
7 Fishing
8 Footpaths
9 Seaside resorts
10 Piers and entertainments
11 Caravan and camping site
12 Nature reserves
13 Untreated sewage disposal
14 Beaches

© DIAGRAM

ENVIRONMENT
Pollution

AIR

Nuclear testing
Rocket exhausts
Aircraft noise
Industrial toxins
Heat pollution

LAND

Noise
Agricultural chemicals
Road vehicle exhausts
Refuse
Slag heaps from mining

SEA

Oil slicks
Beach pollution
Industrial waste and sewage
Waste discharge at sea
Ship wrecks

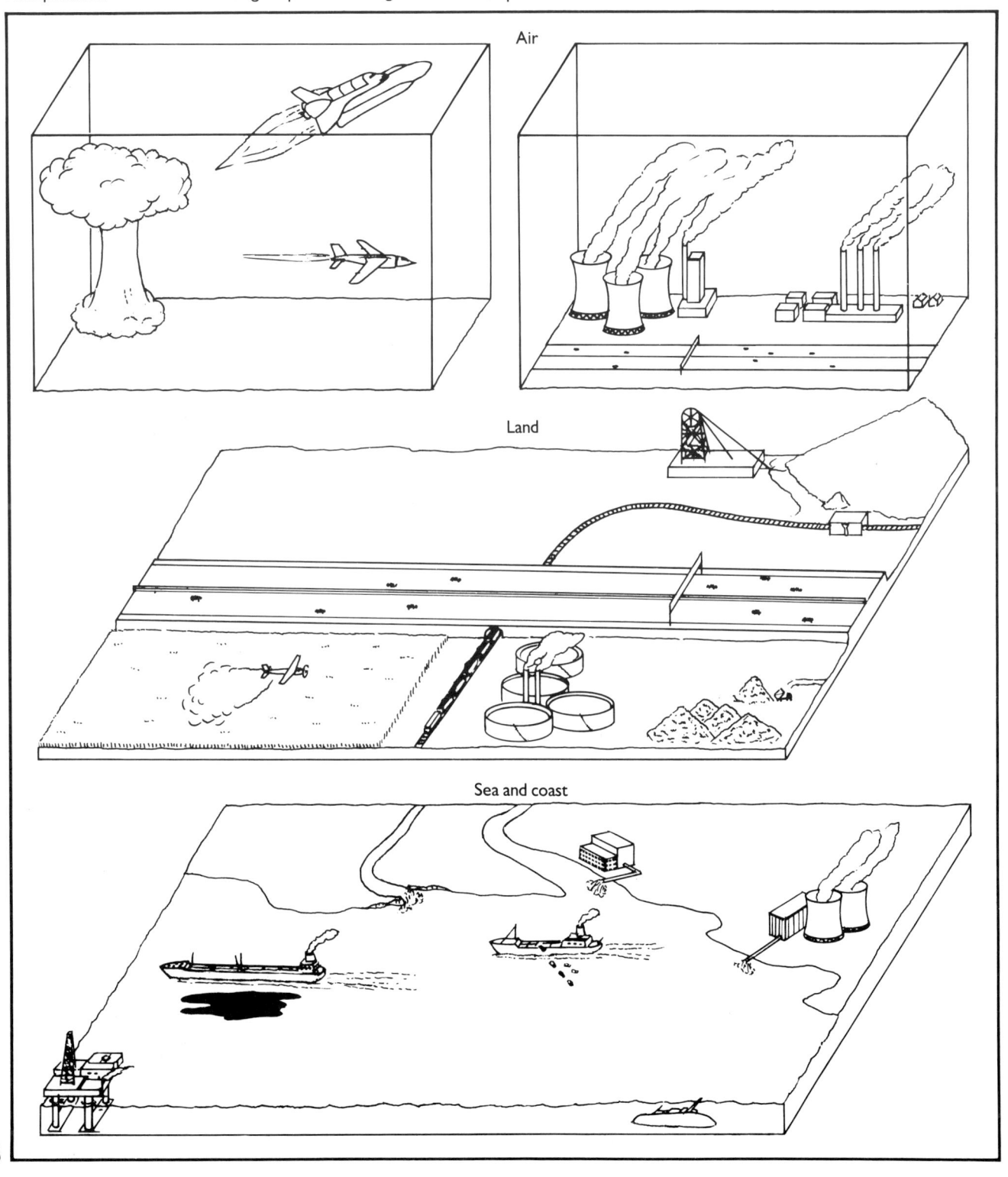

Air

Land

Sea and coast

ENVIRONMENT
Forest reserves and depletion

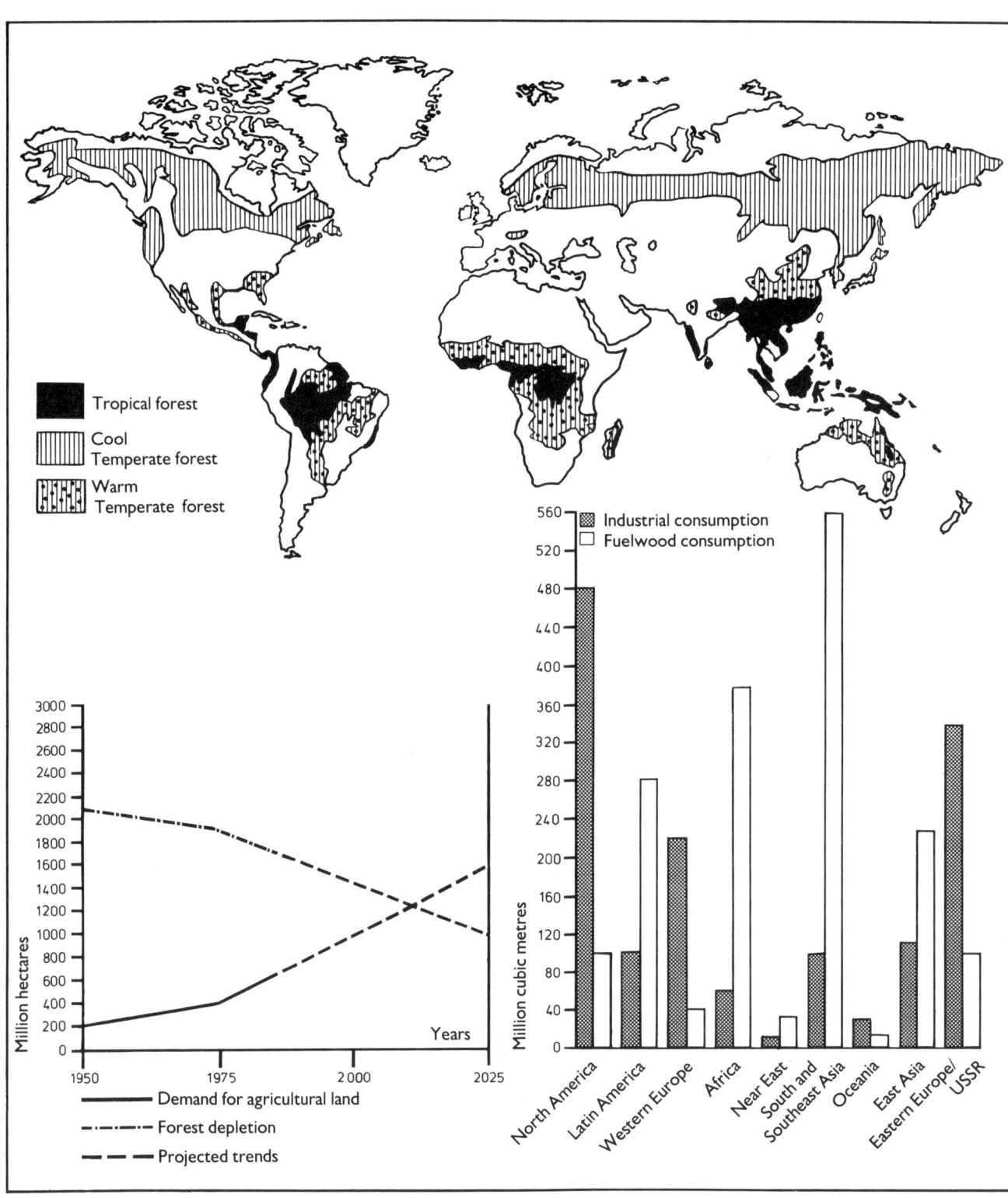

Tropical forest

Cool Temperate forest

Warm Temperate forest

Industrial consumption
Fuelwood consumption

Million cubic metres

560
520
480
440
400
360
320
280
240
200
160
120
80
40
0

North America
Latin America
Western Europe
Africa
Near East
South and Southeast Asia
Oceania
East Asia
Eastern Europe/ USSR

Million hectares

3000
2800
2600
2400
2200
2000
1800
1600
1400
1200
1000
800
600
400
200
0

1950   1975   2000   2025

Years

—————— Demand for agricultural land

—·—·—·— Forest depletion

— — — — Projected trends

©DIAGRAM

ENVIRONMENT
Desertification and its causes

1 Downslope ploughing
2 Monoculture
3 Unprotected fields
4 Poorly managed pasture

5 Deforestation
6 Mudbank
7 Flooded village
8 Gulley erosion

9 Broken bridge
10 Urban slum
11 Landslip
12 Reduced fish catch in shallow water

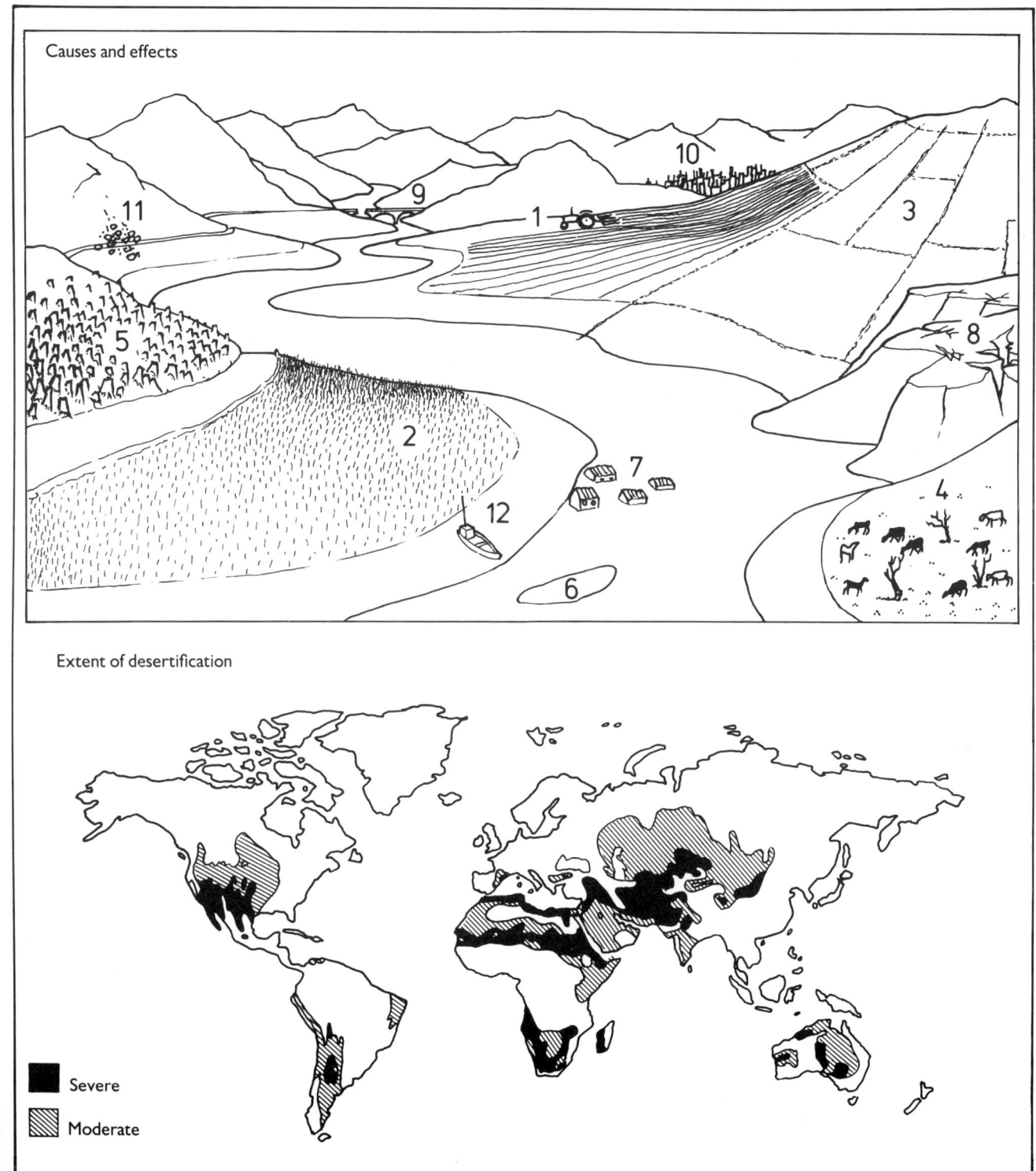

Causes and effects

Extent of desertification

■ Severe

▨ Moderate

©DIAGRAM

INDEX